M000074658

Jessie Faerber is a youth mini where she lives with her husband, Robbie. She is the founder of a project called 'Belle', which is passionate about girls realizing their true value, beauty and purpose through workshops in schools and youth groups. She is enthusiastic about journeying with girls, being real and authentic with her own story and embracing all that Belle is in God's master plan.

MORE THAN JUST PRETTY

JESSIE FAERBER

First published in Great Britain in 2018

Society for Promoting Christian Knowledge
36 Causton Street
London SW1P 4ST
www.spck.org.uk

Copyright © Jessie Faerber 2018

All rights reserved. No part of this book may be reproduced or transmitted in any form or by any means, electronic or mechanical, including photocopying, recording, or by any information storage and retrieval system, without permission in writing from the publisher.

SPCK does not necessarily endorse the individual views contained in its publications.

The author and publisher have made every effort to ensure that the external website and email addresses included in this book are correct and up to date at the time of going to press. The author and publisher are not responsible for the content, quality or continuing accessibility of the sites.

Unless otherwise noted, Scripture quotations are taken from the Holy Bible, New International Version Anglicized. Copyright © 1979, 1984, 2011 Biblica. Used by permission of Hodder & Stoughton Ltd, an Hachette UK company. All rights reserved.
'NIV' is a registered trademark of Biblica.
UK trademark number 1448790.

Some quotations in this publication are from *THE MESSAGE*. Copyright © by Eugene H. Peterson 1993, 1994, 1995, 1996, 2000, 2001, 2002. Used by permission of NavPress. All rights reserved. Represented by Tyndale House Publishers, Inc.

The quotation from Ephesians 2.10 is adapted from the *Holy Bible*, New Living Translation, copyright © 1996. Used by permission of Tyndale House Publishers, Inc., Wheaton, Illinois 60189, USA. All rights reserved.

The publisher and author acknowledge with thanks permission to reproduce extracts from the following:
Philippa Hanna, 'I am amazing'
Permission to reproduce 'Never trust a mirror' has been sought from Erin Hanson.
The quotation by Dallas Willard is copyright © Dallas Willard. Used by permission of the Willard Family Trust.
Every effort has been made to seek permission to use copyright material reproduced in this book. The publisher apologizes for those cases where permission might not have been sought and, if notified, will formally seek permission at the earliest opportunity.

British Library Cataloguing-in-Publication Data
A catalogue record for this book is available from the British Library

ISBN 978–0–281–07786–1
eBook ISBN 978–0–281–07787–8

Typeset by Geethik, India
First printed in Great Britain by Jellyfish Print Solutions
Subsequently digitally reprinted in Great Britain

eBook by Geethik, India

Produced on paper from sustainable forests

To my teenage self, who desperately needed a book like this

To your teenage self, on whom I hope and pray a book like this has a great impact

Hey, lovely. This book was written for the girl who's trying to figure out who she is. This book was written for the girl who looks in the mirror and hates what she sees, worries too much about what she sees or doesn't see that she is so much more than what she sees. This book was written for the girl of no faith, the girl of the Christian faith and the girl of another faith. This book was written for the crazy girl, the quiet girl, the confused girl, the worried girl, the happy girl. You name it. This book was written to help you discover the truth about who you are despite the world's obsession with image! This book was written for you because your story matters. You matter.

This book was written by a girl, a very normal girl. A girl who has a passion to see girls discover their true value, beauty and purpose! Let's rise together. Let's empower one another. Let's explore together. Let's discover how we are #MoreThanJustPretty.

I'm excited for what you will realize about yourself and the impact it will have on your beautiful journey of LIFE.

Your friend, big-sister-type figure,

Jessie

So. Read this book with an open heart. Take your time. Buy a pretty, cool, new little journal and jot down anything that you know you'll need to remind yourself about. Jot down quotes/ideas/and anything else that may or may not knock your socks off. Or draw pictures (that's always fun!). Grab your set of colouring or calligraphy pens and make each page YOURS. Join the virtual conversation on the hashtag . . . wait for it . . . #MoreThanJustPretty. And start your own real-life conversations with your sister, mum, dad, carer, friend, youth group, school, teacher, cousin, mentor . . . anyone! This book is meant to be like going to the supermarket and buying a chocolate bar rather than a bag of apples (this analogy only actually works if you don't like apples that much . . .). What I mean is that my hope is that you will LOVE reading this book; you'll be excited to pick it up and dig into it! So enjoy it and treasure every last word, page and chapter – because they were intricately designed and chosen down to every last detail for YOU.

Shall we commence?

Ready. Set. Go!

CONTENTS

CONTENTS

ACKNOWLEDGEMENTS

Thank you, Robbie, for getting excited when I reported how much I managed to write each day that I sat down at my laptop to create this book (even when I only managed a hundred words). Thank you for celebrating the little wins with me and knowing exactly what to say when the wins definitely weren't happening! The fact you proposed to me mid-writing phase is a very special thought. Thank you for embracing this crazy book adventure and for always championing girls and women alongside me. Thank you for loving Jesus just as much as I do.

Thank you, Mum, for sending me cards of encouragement that arrived miraculously at exactly the time I needed them. Thank you for being one of the greatest prayer warriors behind this book. Thank you for journeying with me in my insecurities over life, image and purpose, and for never saying they were stupid or to get over them. Thank you for walking, carrying and crying me through the other side of them. Thank you for always reminding me about the point of this book: God communicating his love for girls.

Thank you, Faerber family (Dad and Bex), for influencing every part of who I am. Thank you for loving me and having my back. Thank you for bringing me up, for doing life with me and for being such rocks. Thank you for all the adventures that we've had so far (and for the many that are yet to come).

Thank you to my friends who make life an absolute joy and pleasure and make me laugh until my stomach hurts. It hasn't always been easy, but the hardships have subsequently created a strength and a depth in our relationships, and for that, I am so thankful.

Thank you to all those who have influenced me in ministry, faith and life: you must know who you are!

To mention but a few, thank you to the Tolmans for taking me into your family and showing me what a life of ministry is all about and sparking a dream within me.

Also, thank you Mark Griffiths for calling out my strengths, being excited about my dreams with me and pointing me in the right direction.

Thank you to St Peter's Church in Warfield for showing me the importance of doing life together with people. Lifelong family friends have resulted from my upbringing at such a family-orientated church (that's you, Harman family!).

Thank you to St Mellitus College for grounding my ministry in theology and drawing alongside inspiring people who taught me tons. Thank you for introducing me to lifelong friends who are smashing it in youth ministry.

Thank you to New Wine for being the place where I go to serve during the summer and the place where I am fed by faith-shaking, spirit-inspired teaching and communities.

Thank you to the community of St Michael's Church in Southfields for celebrating women in leadership, creating a role for me and for being the place where I worship and feel that I can be my true self.

To all the female empowerers out there (whether in the form of mothers, fathers, carers, siblings, friends, youth workers, magazine writers, charity starters, vicars, teachers, mentors, social media influencers . . .) – KEEP GOING, please. There is a shift happening for such a time as this. Let's keep praying passionately for freedom for girls and women. Let's keep speaking out when we need to speak out. Let's keep speaking truth. Let's keep mentoring, supporting, teaching and role-modelling. On behalf of girls in the years to come – THANK YOU.

To all the people who have spoken to me about Jesus – thank you for speaking truth, life and hope into me.

My prayer is that this book contains words through which God will speak to you, just as all of these people whom I have thanked (and the others that I haven't) have spoken words into my life that have come from God.

So finally, thank YOU for picking up this book (however it has ended up in your hands!) and I pray that the words spread across the pages influence, encourage and have an impact on YOU.

PROLOGUE

GETTING TO KNOW ME QUIZ

You may have bought this book for yourself or your mum/grandma/mentor/youth worker/school may have placed it in your hands and you're wondering who the heck I am and thinking that I have NO CLUE what you're facing! Stay with me, and I think you'll realize that, in some areas, I'm not all that different from you. This book will uncover the truth about some of my story and my 'experience' as well as the story and experiences of other girls like you and me.

But first, to help you get to know me better, I thought a delightful place to start would be with a little quiz. It will help you frame an idea about who it is talking to you through this book (if you don't know already), and it's a bit of fun, right?!

The questions are below, so get out that journal and jot down the options that best describe YOU. Then, towards the end of this section, you should find my personal, carefully calculated answers with which to compare!

QUIZ

1. Your morning buzzzzz:
   - ☆ Tea
   - ☆ Coffee
   - ☆ Orange juice
   - ☆ None of the above.

2. Which kinda person are ya?
   - ☆ Dogs
   - ☆ Cats.

3. What colour eyes do you have?
   - ☆ Blue
   - ☆ Acorn
   - ☆ Grey
   - ☆ Green
   - ☆ Other (if that's possible . . .).

4. Thoughts?
   - ☆ I'm a Christian.
   - ☆ I'm an 'atheist'.
   - ☆ I don't really know.
   - ☆ I follow another faith.
   - ☆ I'm open to ideas.

5. OK, so which would you choose?
   - ☆ Lindt
   - ☆ Galaxy (with cookie bits)
   - ☆ The classic Dairy Milk

- ☆ Mars Bar
- ☆ Malteasers
- ☆ Other (because I could carry on but it would take up A LOT of pages).

6 Choices . . . choices . . . choices
- ☆ *The Lion King*
- ☆ *The Little Mermaid*
- ☆ *Cinderella*
- ☆ *Frozen.*

7 Do you like who you are?
- ☆ Yes
- ☆ No
- ☆ It's complicated
- ☆ Sometimes.

8 Which one?!
- ☆ Books
- ☆ Films.

IT'S ANSWERS TIME (!) . . .

1 Your morning buzzzzz:
- ☆ Coffee – probs not a good thing. If I were to be more specific: a vanilla latte.

2 Which kinda person are ya?
- ☆ Dogs – because I want a husky.
- ☆ Cats – because I have a gorgeous ginger cat called George

(kinda cheating).

3 What colour eyes do you have?
- ☆ Acorn – because 'brown' sounds more boring (ha).

4 Thoughts?
- ☆ I'm a Christian – it's massively helped me on my journey but it doesn't mean it's the only answer and it doesn't mean I'm not accepting of other faiths and beliefs. You're all fab.

5 OK, so which would you choose?
- ☆ Galaxy (with cookie bits)
- ☆ Malteasers

I couldn't possibly choose between the two . . .

6 Choices . . . choices . . . choices
- ☆ *Frozen* – I'm (always) surprisingly not a big fan of animation but *Frozen* stole my heart. I want to be Elsa.

7 Do you like who you are?
- ☆ Yes – although, at times I would fluctuate between all four options because that's life, eh? Or is it? It's been a long journey to get to where I am today. And I pray that this book is in the hands of someone who needs to hear the truth about who she is.

8 Which one?!
- ☆ Books – if you'd have asked me a few years ago I would have said 'films' but now defo books. And I promise I'm not just saying that because this is a book . . .

PS: if you put 'films', I promise I won't be offended . . . let's hope you and this book become friends . . .

Hopefully you had *some* fun there! Oh, and hopefully it was relatively insightful to stop and have a think about who you are, and perhaps learn just a *little* about me! I'm intrigued as to how our answers may compare . . .

Anyhow. Probably best to get on with it now.

VALUE

There are many things we put our value in in this world. This chapter aims to explore what these different things are, from the people we know to how we look. My hope is that it will unlock some realities for you so that your perception about who you are becomes less and less distorted and more and more truthful.

Bring it on!

AM I WHO I KNOW?

One of the things I LOVE, because it always intrigues me, is psychology. Now, don't lose me at the first proper page of this book (!) . . . It's actually cool because it explains all about the human mind: our actions, thoughts and behaviour!

Psychologists say that our identity is 'socially constructed', meaning that it's formed in our social contexts. Think about your contexts in the list below and think about the people in your life, and how they all merge together in order to influence our identity.

Friends
School
Family
Faith
Media
Location
Social
Youth
Ethnicity
Other

This is why we're taking up some pages to explore a little bit of why the people we choose to have in our lives do have an IMPACT.

'We are family' (I literally sing the song whenever I read this title)

I'm lucky enough to have grown up in a family whom I love very much and who have treated me very well. I want you to understand that I know this isn't always the case. What I also want you to understand is HOW my family has shaped who I am and, in turn, reflect sensitively on both the positive and negative ways your family has shaped who you are, too.

My mum is very much a gentle, creative girly-girl and my dad is a logical, organized hard worker. As you'd expect, I've turned out to be a mixture of the two of them! But I think this truth is something we don't always fully realize.

When I finished school I spent my gap year interning in Wollongong, Australia. While I was there I worked for an incredible woman called Tammy and lived with her and her family. The year was formational on many fronts, but one aspect that sticks out in my memory is them banning some of my language! I'd picked up my mum's character trait of 'gentleness', yet it just so happened that in my life it outworked itself in people-pleasing. I was so conscious about making other people happy and not overstating my opinions that I answered, 'I don't mind' or 'It's up to you', or any other combination of the words, to questions thrown in my direction. It literally could be any question, e.g. 'What do you want for dinner?' Tammy consequently banned phrases of this kind from my vocabulary!

Once I was unable to say these things, I found it reshaped the way I thought about the value of what I had to put into conversation. It encouraged me to explore and shape my true beliefs and opinions without fear of what other people would think and in so doing I found my unique and powerful voice, a voice that wanted to be listened to and heard.

'Friends are the family we choose'

If someone were to ask me about my experience of friends in secondary school then my mind would take me back to an experience I had in the summer before year 9. As I started secondary school, I tasked myself with becoming a part of the 'popular crew' (a cringe phrase but the easiest way to determine what I'm talking about). After much striving, I made it. I was ecstatic to know that my identity was wrapped up in

The attitude we have towards ourselves is by far the most important of all our attitudes the identity of the other girls in the group. I was cool. People should like me. Boys would fancy me.

I have the delight of being a summer baby, so for my birthday that summertime I planned on having a big inflatable jousting set in the back garden for all to be impressed by and enjoy. Unfortunately the British weather was unreliable. So, bowling had to suffice!! The evening ahead involved bullying within the walls of my own home. It continued into the first few weeks of school in year 9: I vividly remember an object of some sort being thrown precisely in my direction on the school field. It broke me. I was left feeling like a nuisance, insignificant, valueless.

Maybe some of those words resonate with how you feel? Or maybe some other words come to mind for you?

Did you notice that my experience all started with putting my value in popularity?

It may be that your situation at school was worse. It may be that it was better. We all have different encounters with different people but each encounter has the opportunity to shape who we think we are AND who we're likely to become.

With the power of hindsight, I can see that how the people in my life (at school) made me *feel* about who I was quickly morphed into who I thought I was. Do you see the difference? My perception about myself was distorted by my perception of what other people thought about me through how they treated me.

When our opinions about ourselves are distorted, we start to believe a distorted truth about who we are (i.e. a lie) and I can see this so clearly in how the whole situation panned out. I thought that without popularity I would be empty and useless. Yet once I achieved popularity I was left feeling empty and useless. A distorted opinion led to a distorted truth. A bit of a lose–lose, right?!

People are a gift. People are constantly entering and leaving our lives and yet, as you've seen, each one has the ability to shape us for better or for worse. Choose wisely. You'll hear me repeating again and again how *awareness = action!* The two are intrinsically linked. What I mean by this is that once we're aware of something, it inevitably leads us to act differently in some way. Awareness drives us to create some kind of change in our lives or with ourselves. We'll explore more of this very soon.

Teenhood sweethearts (as opposed to childhood sweethearts . . .)

One promise that I have to make to you and to myself is that I am not going to get all cringey and weird talking about CRUSHES. There are just a few things I want to iron out for you because I think they are a MUST-KNOW.

Often, as we 'grow up' we're trying to make sense of ourselves and how we fit into the world. And sometimes we feel rubbish about ourselves (it's a normal feeling to feel at times, I assure you). One of the key things that society tells us is that gaining a partner will fill the hole that makes us feel rubbish and life will be a wonderful fairy-tale of romance and flowers and chocolate. We see this through TV, film, social media, friends – everywhere we look.

Think all the way back to Barbie and Ken and how we immediately associate one with the other. Think back to the fairy-tales you used to (and may still!) watch and how the 'happily ever after' was only reached with true love's kiss from some kind of knight in shining armour. Think about the last pop song you listened to and how it's likely to be written about love in some way or another. This idea that we need a partner (or 'another half') to complete us is EVERYWHERE.

But *don't fret, my friends*. Luckily, I've been there and done it. I used to get on a lot better with boys because my metaphorical walls were up so high when it came to girls, so I totally understand that guy friends are FAB. But here's a little advice.

Gloria Steinem is an American feminist and journalist and she says this:

> **Far too many people are looking for the right person, instead of trying to be the right person.**

You're amazing. You have your whole life ahead of you. You have dreams, passions and goals. I'm not gonna get all 'you don't need no man' because one day it will become a matter of want over need. But what you will never *need* is 'another half'. You are a whole in yourself. In my experience, taking time to just BE YOU is the most self-fulfilling, confidence-building choice you can make and action you can implement, HONESTLY. If you can't be yourself without a partner, you won't be yourself *with* a partner. And being yourself is vital for the whole of life.

Sticks and stones

Probably the main reason other people influence what we think about ourselves so much is because of the words that they say to us. We're talking about how important it is to be ourselves and to value ourselves, but we need to understand the devastating impact that words can have and how to navigate them.

Psychologists also say that our thoughts about who we are revolve around our ideas of what others think about us. For example, other girls in year 9 made me feel useless and insignificant, which then became an idea I believed to be true about myself. We know that the phrase 'sticks and stones can break my bones but words can never hurt me' isn't legit because words can cut our souls.

I know that I've had words spoken over me such as 'boring'. Sounds lame, right?! But even now, if for example my sister is joking around and utters the phrase 'You're boring', it cuts me inside. This was an insult thrown my way in my younger years, and even now I have to call time and explain to her that it has such negative emotional connotations that I need her to take it back! (She would never mean it meanly anyway.)

Another word that people used to brand me with was 'shy'. You may or may not know that I spent three years studying for a degree in theology and youth ministry. It basically meant three years studying and essay-writing about God stuff and youth stuff with a bunch of inspiring college mates and lecturers. ANYWAY. I remember a particular Monday morning, aka the first time I met the five other people I'd be journeying the next three years with. Thoughts were racing through my head. How should I act? What should I say? What if they don't like me? I'm really shy and stuff so how should I play this?

By the end of the day I'd never felt more myself. I realized I'd been nothing close to 'shy' – what did that mean, anyway?! It began a process of reflection for me: a good reflection, not a boring one. I realized that during my childhood someone had spoken the word 'shy' over me repeatedly. I realized I had grabbed that mask and worn it for many years. I carried 'shy' for so long that it started to define who I was and how I approached different situations. I would immediately cave in. But that wasn't me. I realized at that point I had the choice to let the power behind the word 'shy' disintegrate. I'm open, I'm chatty, I'm passionate, I'm loved, I'm significant, I'm confident. I'm learning to own who I am. Love it. Embrace it. Choose what you let define you.

What words do you think describe you?

Negative words

As I mentioned, two words used to describe me were 'boring' and 'shy'. I let these words define me, and yet it wasn't at all who I was. Here's where the awareness equation kicks in again

Words only have POWER when they become what we think of OURSELVES about who we are

Brené Brown

(awareness = action). By being aware that someone is speaking insulting words about you and by being aware that you don't have to carry those false words any more, you inevitably change the extent to which you allow that person to play a role in your life and begin the process of letting go of what was said.

(CUE – 'Let it go' by Elsa).

Tips and tricks

- ☆ Take a moment to write down those negative words that have been spoken over you and scrunch them up tight in your fist before throwing them away. They don't define you.

Positive words

Just as negative words have the power to break us down, positive words can build us up. Being aware that words have power changes the attitude with which we use our words.

Tips and tricks

- ☆ Take a moment to encourage someone today.
- ☆ Take a moment to tell a family member what you love about him or her.

Ultimately, other people saying something about us doesn't mean it's true just because they say it. Not one bit. This is why it's so important to know who we are inside and out. It means that with any words thrown our way, we get to assess them against what we KNOW is true about ourselves, and if it isn't in line with these things then we can scribble it out. And yes, it's a process, but every little step will make it more ingrained into our natural way of thinking/doing things.

Recently, I've been thinking about the difference between the words we speak to ourselves and the words we speak to our mates. If I were to write down some of the negative words that used to cross my mind throughout the day, the list would be the following:

Ugly
Useless
Insignificant
Lanky
Etc.

Yet I would NEVER speak those things to my best mate. Imagine if I did!! The point I'm trying to make here is that the words we speak to ourselves aren't always kind. What if we were to speak to ourselves just as we'd speak to a friend?

The words we speak and the words we latch onto are like the hands of a potter on wet clay: they mould and shape our character and our life.

But let me tell you something: the words of others only have power when we let them. Words do NOT have to define you. Words do NOT have the last say about who you are.

AM I WHAT I ACHIEVE?

School. We all have different experiences at school, don't we?

I did some research:

Primary school children generally spend about 779 hours in the classroom every year and secondary school 'young people' (because you're no longer children, according to me) spend around 656 hours at school every year.[1] This means we spend about 10,045 hours at school in total over our lifetime. They look like crazy numbers, especially considering they're only every YEAR.

That sounds like a crazy amount of time, right?!

HOWEVER. The average life expectancy is 75 years, which means that we will live on this Earth for around 657,450 hours.

Now what does that make you think?

You may be somewhere between thinking that you spend a heck of a lot of time at school or slightly bewildered by how you'll spend the 647,000ish other hours of life.

The thing is that, right now, school is your world. And I get it. I did school. I've been there. And it is a vital part of life, a blessing, a privilege that we get to 'enjoy'. You're also at school during your most formative years. Although your brain is learning so many new things, your whole being is also forming. A changing brain means a changing identity.

You may find yourself asking questions such as:

What am I good for?
How can I be liked by other people?
What is my unique stamp on the world?
How far can I push myself?
How far can I rebel?

So, although your school years are forming your world, there is *so* much more to come.

As I mentor girls tackling their secondary school world, there is one thing that always comes back to haunt me. It's this ingrained lie that 'who you are is what you achieve'. The majority of us are pressured on every side to achieve the grades we 'need' because otherwise we enter a spiral of self-doubt, insecurity and a good-for-nothing mentality.

Girls, we were each designed with the innate desire to pursue dreams, to learn and to explore our unique potential. Many of us will achieve far more than we could ever imagine. BUT: who you are does not start or stop there.

At school, I placed so much of who I was in my achievements. I strived for the highest grades, the commendations, the merits and to be the best. If I was achieving great things, I was content in myself. And, yes, we should celebrate great things and there's nothing wrong with that. But it will get to a point when these things cannot sustain us any longer. We run faster, harder, longer on the treadmill and we never see the top of the ladder. We have to be content in ourselves as we are: failures, mistakes, accolades, triumphs.

Just know that school isn't life. It's only for such a time as this. Try to enjoy it, challenge yourself and grow in learning all about who you are: your passions, dislikes, character and ability. See it as a stepping stone to whatever is next for you. Seeing the big picture allows us to treasure the smaller details.

AM I WHAT I LOOK LIKE?

Every morning I would wake up and look in the mirror. I'd scan my face and my stomach would sink with hate at what I saw. Every morning I would wake up and look in the mirror and proceed to make myself over. Make-up was my saviour. It made me feel better about myself. But also worse about myself, because I knew my 'new face' technically wasn't me. I longed to like what I saw in the mirror but the hate just spiralled and spiralled until a conversation was sparked by someone asking, 'Jessie. Do you think you're beautiful?' I wonder what you'd say if someone asked you that exact question: 'Do you think you're beautiful?'

This world is so incredibly image-saturated. By that I mean that we are confronted with images left, right and centre! Think of TV, magazines, social media, advertising hoardings, etc. This has sparked our obsession with image. Although I do think it's great that we care, I think we have to be SO careful that it doesn't become our life's obsession. We have to be careful that who we are doesn't become what we look like, *because that's deception at its very best . . .*

Do you remember when you stopped loving the way that you look? Why did your attitude change?

The most **important** thing in your life is not what you do; it's **who you become**. That's what you will take into **eternity**

Dallas Willard

Recently, I gave up make-up for the duration of Lent because I wanted to prove that who we are isn't defined by how we look, I wanted to be an example to other girls and I wanted to become more comfortable in my own skin.

It was HARD! I journalled and blogged my experience, so I thought I should share with you some of the thoughts I had after only four days:

- Is it too late to back out?
- What if people think I'm ill or haven't slept in days or something?
- I fancy wearing lipstick today – oh, wait . . .
- I hate this.
- I can't fail because then I'd be a hypocrite.
- I wish contouring hadn't yet been introduced.
- At least my face is relatively clear at the moment (*touch wood*).
- What if people treat me differently?
- Ooooh I might buy this new eyebrow pencil – oh, wait . . .
- 40 days . . . that's almost two whole months . . .

Again, it was HARD! But I DID IT. And yes, I may now sound old and strange: I learned so much.

I realized that the fact that I wasn't wearing make-up didn't make me any less myself. I was still the laid-back, lacking-common-sense, funny, smiley, caring Jessie that I was with make-up. Beyond that, I realized that we are so much more than our image. And yet our image is the thing that we really strive for compliments on. Why?

There's a poem I absolutely love by rupi kaur that articulates this truth beautifully.[2] In it, she apologizes for having sometimes thought of women as pretty when she could have described them another way, like brave or intelligent. What a woman has done or endured says far more about her than just what she was born with. It's fine to be pretty, but there's so much more to someone than that.

I realized that I wanted to be more than just my image. I don't want to be 'just pretty'. I want to be pretty resilient, pretty wise, pretty faithful, pretty loving and pretty brave. All those things will make us extraordinary girls.

I realized that I didn't need to rely on make-up to sustain me. I became more comfortable in my own skin and proud of my natural self.

How does this makes you feel?
How much time and energy do you put into making yourself look a certain way?

You are so much more than that.

There are people around the world who have nothing. I always wonder about them. Do you think they mind what they see in the mirror? Perhaps they don't even own one! We are lucky, you and me.

Did you know that according to Meaghan Ramsey, previous Global Director of the Dove Self-Esteem Project, *10,000 people Google every month, 'Am I ugly?'* YouTube is flooded with girls posting videos of themselves asking that exact question to an audience of strangers. To put a number on it, 850,000 girls have posted a video such as this.

Girls seem to no longer love what they see in the mirror. Scrap that. Girls seem to no longer even like what they see in the mirror. Girls seem to no longer be able to identify themselves as beautiful, but need the affirmation of other people.

Do you? Why is this?

As a society, we've torn away from valuing people's character. Some of the most beautiful people I know are beautiful because they radiate such self-confidence that doesn't rely on their image. They're beautiful because they know who they are: their passions and dreams. They're beautiful because they care about other people more than themselves. They're beautiful because they're adventurous in the way they live life.

I want that kind of beauty. Not what society deems 'beautiful'. Not what social media says is 'sexy'. Not what requires other people's opinions.

Now, I must add that this is a lifelong journey. There are days when I feel I look so rubbish and therefore feel so rubbish that my whole day just goes . . . guess what . . . rubbish. Silly, huh? I find myself retracing my steps to figure out what happened along the way, and I find myself doing a lot of self-talk to steer back to making a little bit more sense.

Pause. SELF-TALK – what do I mean?

I want to be more
than just pretty

I'm talking about those moments when we're aware that what we are thinking about ourselves (or others, for that matter) isn't quite true, and we desire to build ourselves back up again. These times are VITAL for our emotional health, girls. And, as I said, it all starts with the awareness.

Imagine I go to the bathroom in the middle of a work (or school) day and catch my reflection in the mirror and the following thoughts run through my mind: 'You look horrific, very, very bad, how did that even happen, everyone must have noticed, you can't do anything, why are you even trying?'

Do you see the spiral that twirls out of control? Positive self-talk has the same start but a drastically different ending: 'You look horrific, very, very bad, but actually you are so much more than what you look like, no one will even notice, it doesn't even matter at all, you can't look perfect that's impossible for anyone, you have a purpose, you are treasured, you are beautiful, go and smash it today.'

You may be cringing, and that's OK, I cringe at myself all the time. But the power of this is actually life-changing because if you can grab these thoughts as they arise, you can trade them for what is truth-speaking and life-fulfilling and you'll feel UNSTOPPABLE.

As I was thinking about ways we can steer away from unhealthy mentalities and lifestyles, I was reminded that we tend to compliment or encourage one another based on what we look like, i.e. 'I love your hair', 'That outfit looks fierce',

Your value doesn't decrease based on someone's inability to see your worth

'Your make-up is on-point . . .' What if, instead, we steered towards the following:

- ☆ You're so inspiring.
- ☆ I love that you're so down to earth.
- ☆ You make me want to be better.
- ☆ Chatting with you makes me feel great.
- ☆ We need more girls like you.
- ☆ There's something different about you.
- ☆ I love your passion.
- ☆ You're so brave.
- ☆ I love how adventurous you are.

I challenge you to see yourself in a new light. This challenge is a special one because it will influence the way you see the other girls in your life.

Tips and tricks

- ☆ Go a day without wearing make-up.
- ☆ Write an anonymous letter of encouragement to a friend (without mentioning her image), or even just compliment your friends without mentioning their image.

BE YOU

At this point of each section I want to explore the topic through a biblical lens. Don't let that put you off! Give it a go. I'm not going to get too heavy and theological but I will explore what your Creator says about YOU.

My most favourite EVER Bible verse is one that you'll hear about time and time again as we unpack it throughout this book:

> **For you are God's MASTERPIECE, created anew in Christ Jesus to do the good things he planned for you long ago.**
>
> **(Ephesians 2.10)**

Yes, it's a Bible verse. You might love that or it may make you feel uncomfortable, but don't let that warp the truth. I'm going to unpack exactly what this means for you! Basically,

you're a masterpiece

and that's no exaggeration. When we realize that, it changes everything! I promise you!

So, let's go back over what we've explored in this chapter but not quite the same way. Instead, let's go back over it through the lens of seeing ourselves as a masterpiece.

Am I who I know?

A couple of years ago I attended a few events that were discussing the pressures and expectations of the twenty-first-century girl. What struck me most was that we have actually created and sustained a culture where it's become normal to slate and discourage other girls. Competition creeps up from every corner.

Yet Jesus entered into the culture of his time and transformed it by being an encourager. He spent time with the outcast, the lost and the alone. That didn't make *him* outcast, lost and alone. Jesus transformed culture by encouraging all those he spent time with – he totally eradicated negativity when talking to and talking about other people. If we take the Bible verse for what it says, then it means *I* am a masterpiece and it means that *you* are a masterpiece. Do you see my point? The outcast, the lost and the alone aren't excluded from being masterpieces.

We need to support and love one another. We need to be real community rather than virtual community. We need to come alongside those younger than us. We need to fight for one another.

There are countless verses in the Bible commanding us to be encouragers. Let's be countercultural in our approach to other people, knowing that our value is not determined by other people but that we can use our words to make others feel valued.

Am I what I achieve?

Girls. I spent the majority of my time in school trying to achieve approval and value from others. I was addicted to the affirmation I would gain from my parents, teachers and friends and my identity was founded on it. What I didn't realize was how suffocating it was. It's something I've also journeyed through while doing my degree. A bad grade would send me spiralling into self-hatred and a good grade would sustain me for at least a couple of hours (yup, it was that fleeting).

Ephesians 2.10 says that you're a masterpiece. That means that you are a masterpiece. It doesn't mean that if you achieve and achieve and strive and strive then you'll be a masterpiece. Your value and identity aren't found in what you do but in who you are. 'I AM' comes before 'I DO'.

This doesn't mean that we can't achieve and do great things. It just means that those things don't define us. We are valuable no matter what.

Am I how I look?

You'll hear me bang on about this a lot throughout the book but it's totally VITAL to get our heads around.

When I think of the image of a masterpiece I know that what makes it a masterpiece is not just what it looks like on the surface. I did a little bit of an internet search to see what people take into account when judging art across the country and I found a ton of criteria: skill, technique, creativity, originality, imagination, love, patience, time, artistic equipment and perseverance.

I spent the majority of life basing my value on what I looked like. When I realized that it was totally warped I felt pretty lost. You may be feeling lost as you read all of this, and that's OK, please don't worry! One of the main things I've learned is that a masterpiece is a masterpiece because of the skill, technique, creativity, originality, imagination, love, patience, time, artistic equipment and perseverance of its master. Our master is God.

'Master' doesn't mean controlling, dominating and rule-based in this case. It highlights the inherent worth that God places on each of us: his precious, adored, significant creations. We are valued because we are his.

Sticks and stones

God's thoughts about you (and me) are greater, truer and more powerful than your thoughts about yourself. And they are greater, truer and more powerful than other people's thoughts about you.

We have to allow *his* words (not our own, or the words of others) to press against the wet clay of our soul and shape us. Words in the Bible are formational in the way we see God, ourselves and others around us.

Which story?

Culture will say that who we know, what we achieve, what we look like and what others say about us is all true and justified. We live in the tension between the world saying we aren't good enough and our God saying we're enough as we are. We live in the tension between the world saying we aren't doing enough and God saying that it's who we are, not what we do, that is central to the self. We live in the tension between the world pointing out our shortcomings and God rejoicing in us moment by moment.

God's master-story enables us to FULLY embrace our call as masterpieces. Our choice to live within the worldly or master-

You KNOW me

inside and out,

and you know

EVERY BONE in my body;

You know EXACTLY how I was made,

bit by bit, how I was

sculpted from NOTHING

into SOMETHING

Psalm 139.15, The Message

story will have an impact on the ordinary or extraordinary lives that we lead.

Which story do you choose to live in? After having tried to live in a certain way, I'm a believer that if we choose the worldly story, we live a life of constantly trying to keep up and never being fully satisfied. We were created to be a part of a story bigger than us; we have been called to more than this. Our value is steeped in the fact that we are a part of God's master-story.

When we decide which story we want to be a part of, we gain the authority to decide what we allow to become a part of our story or not. We gain the authority to speak life and truth into all circumstances. And that's EXCITING!

God's words about the value of who we are will never cease to amaze me! He looks at you, his daughter, and he proclaims, 'YOU ARE MY DAUGHTER WHOM I LOVE.'

If something about what this book is exploring is stirring up an excitement within you and you want to know more of it, then why not say this little prayer:

> Dear God, I understand that I am your daughter. I understand that you created me and that you love me just the way I am. I want to be a part of your master-story, and I'm sorry for all the things that have got in the way. I commit my life to you and I want to have a personal relationship with you. I want to walk with you in freedom and truth for the rest of my life. Amen.

BEAUTY

AM I ENOUGH?

One of the questions that I find I ask myself on a frequent basis is AM I ENOUGH? It's amazing how painful such a question can be. There have been days where I feel so useless it's hard to even get out of bed and try to attempt the day. There have been times when I go clothes shopping and stare in the changing-room mirrors hating the imperfect image in front of me.

We've already explored how we are more than our image, but I think we need to delve into this world of image a little more to fully grasp the ins and outs of it.

All things 'girly'

I wonder what pops up on your iPhone or laptop when you search 'toys for girls'? For starters, it's FULL of pink things. Can I just say, it's OK if you don't like pink. Shock, horror, right?! Growing up, I used to associate pink with being a girl, and that's kind of not OK. I mean, THERE ARE SO MANY OTHER COLOURS OUT THERE.

Dolls

Next, you will notice that there are a lot of doll-type figures. You may remember them being the pinnacle of childhood playtime. I mean, I used to love my Barbie and Bratz dolls and recall hours on end creating little dramas with them with my sister in the playroom. I used to love it, for sure. The doll has been present in childhood for thousands of years. The thing is that advertising in our world today has made it possible for a girl to watch *Frozen* while wearing the perfect replica of Elsa's dress and playing with her Elsa doll in matching clothing. The underlying project for a girl then quietly becomes to acquire as many of these items as possible. By this, I mean that we don't realize the strength of advertising that makes it our job to plead our little hearts out until we own the Elsa doll, the matching outfit, the DVD and all the other items the Disney Store sells relating to *Frozen*! I certainly tried to do it!

The doll becomes the image in our mind of 'perfection' from a very early age.

Princesses

The other story that we're told is that we are and can be a PRINCESS. Think of our princess dolls, fairy parties, the dressing-up box at home. For some reason, we've been shaped to imagine that perfection is being princess-like. We're congratulated on our 'becoming pretty'-ness. We're put in princess clothing. We are cooed over about our beauty and cuteness from the moment we are born.

Do you remember any of this:

'Aww, you are such a little princess.'
'What princess would you like to be today?'
'Princesses don't do that.'
'You are Mummy's little princess.'

Now, growing up, I loved this. I always wanted to be the beautiful princess living the fairy-tale, searching for my Prince. I would've done anything to be Mia in *The Princess Diaries* (if you haven't seen that film, stop reading this book right now and go and watch it!). And do you know what, I still think the whole idea is gorgeous – yes, I do.

BUT [keep reading], it's also very dangerous. Why, why, why, I hear you ask.

It's because the princesses we see in films, hold as dolls in our hands and imagine in our heads are totally unattainable. It is a fantasy. And the trouble comes when we let ourselves feel inadequate, useless and not enough because we aren't perfect. To us, this perfection looks like the norm. This is because the images we're surrounded by make us feel like they are the norm when they don't even come close to reality.

Reality check: no one can actually be perfect.

You may be thinking, 'Yeah, but I haven't touched a doll for years and they're plastic. And I don't care about princesses, I understand that it's all fantasy . . . I know that, that's no issue . . .'

I get your point. But the images we refer to as 'perfection' are constantly evolving along with us as we grow up: they never stop. When we outgrow the doll, we find other sources of 'perfection'. And we do all this without even realizing we're doing it. I know people in their 20s and 30s who have never fully grasped that the reason they feel inadequate is because of the societal images of perfection they understood that they have to live up to. I ran a few workshops with college girls and was so surprised by the lack of anyone in their lives who told them that images of perfection in society aren't real. Genuinely, they had never unlocked that conversation before. We looked at pages and pages of adverts, magazines and Instagram pages and debated their reality! This is why it's so important that we understand what is going on in our society and in our heads!

To go back to my little motto, awareness = action. If we understand the messages that society is telling us, we can do something about it.

Models

One of my and my sister's favourite programmes for post-school relaxation was *America's Next Top Model* because we were delighted by the concept of a panel of beautiful people picking out the most beautiful people in the USA. Oh, and we were fascinated by the hairdos, crazy make-up and extravagant outfits. While it's a very entertaining show, it taps into our desire to be beautiful and subconsciously tells us (because of the fact that we're sitting on the sofa, not walking down the catwalk) that beautiful isn't us.

I don't know about you, but I somehow grew up with this underlying thought that if I could be a model then 'I would've made it in this world'. I desperately wanted the swishing hair, the long, toned legs, the perfect complexion and everything else that I guess you gained from the title 'Model'.

This thought came crashing down when I watched a TED talk by Cameron Russell entitled 'Looks aren't everything, believe me, I'm a model'. The video has the capacity to shock and to free girls from false ideas.

Here's one of the things she says:

> **If you're wondering, if I have thinner thighs and shinier hair, will I be happier, you just need to meet a group of models because they have the thinnest thighs, the shiniest hair and the coolest clothes, and [yet] they're the most physically insecure people probably on the planet.**

When I first heard this, I was like, 'Excuse me . . . I've been trying so hard to look like a runway model and now you're telling me that even they aren't happy with how they look?!' Nuts, right?

Does it make it all seem a tad pointless to you like it does to me? If the people in society who are deemed to be the pinnacle of beauty aren't secure in themselves, then surely this whole confidence, self-assurance thing has to do with something other than 'beauty' itself?

In this case, perhaps 'being enough' has nothing to do with what we look like.

Digital-ness (that's a word, right?)

We're going to explore more about how social media comes into play a bit further along in this book. But it's worth mentioning at this point that it has a massive impact upon what it feels like for us to 'be enough'. This is because of the extent to which we are surrounded by and immersed in other people's photos of what we deem 'perfection'.

Oh, and the majority of them are edited, Photoshopped and/or filtered.

'I must look perfect'

Do you know, this whole perfection game is quite an interesting one. I have to say, in my early 20s, it's a very predominant issue. We look at the lives other people create for themselves (usually from what they post on social media) and deem that they've got it all sorted when, really, no one does!

The word 'perfection', according to the reliable (or not so reliable) source called Wikipedia, means: 'a state of completeness and flawlessness'. Different make-up and skin care brands will say that 'flawlessness' is achievable but, my goodness, it is not (marketing is a money-making scheme, remember – they like to profit from our self-doubt and insecurities).

The thing that is really hard, and really amazing, is giving up on being perfect and beginning the work of becoming yourself

Anna Quindlen

There is such beauty in imperfection. There is beauty in the people who I meet who are so OK with their flaws that they ooze confidence and happiness in themselves. Flaws are what make us uniquely us.

It's funny because, as I write this, I'm thinking about the flaws that I see in myself. When I say them out loud I realize how silly they are!

I have a black freckle in the middle of my nose (people mistake it for dirt – it's incredibly awkward every time!!!).
My legs are slightly skewwhiff when I walk.
I have little eyes which get lost when I try to smile.

I'm actually cringing at myself. And I'm kinda stuck now. I'm trying to figure out why there aren't more. I think it's because, yes, there are things I would change if I could (like having slimmer legs, being more tanned and more defined cheekbones (gosh, I feel silly writing them)) but actually they aren't me. I'm no walking image of perfection but I am me. And the most bizarre, but totally true, thing is that these flaws seem gigantic to me but the likelihood is that people around me have never even noticed them, or in their minds they're exactly the things that make me me in the first place. How fantabulous is that?

Let's take the first one on my list. One of my insecurities through school was a dark black freckle that is very central on the top of my nose. The amount of people who thought it was dirt was UNBELIEVABLE. OK, so it was partly believable. Anyhow, when I actually started up a conversation with my friends about it, they explained how much they loved it because it made me me (plus the fact that it's very central is quite satisfying). Now I decide to OWN IT.

You may find that when it comes to thinking about those things you would change about yourself, they are actually a bit silly and would totally mean that you aren't you.

So basically, if we're seeking perfection then, yes, we will never feel like we are enough.

But, if you're seeking to be you, then you're starting from a very good place. If you're seeking to be you, then you're in for the biggest adventure of all.

AM I PRETTY?

The question on the mind of every girl at some point in her life when she looks in the mirror, looks at others, flicks through magazines or goes to bed at night is, 'Am I pretty?' The question ripples across the nation despite age, nationality and ethnicity.

When I was at school, here was a typical day for me:

7.30 a.m. My start to the day was never crazily early (probably because school was a five-minute drive from my house!). Every morning was a make-over morning. I would wake up and put my face on and do my hair. Perching on the edge of my stool at my dressing table, I would analyse my naked face, feeling inadequate and ugly. Fifteen minutes later a transformation had taken place; make-up and hair straighteners were my life-savers.

8.45 a.m. Pre-registration it was likely I would pop to my form group via the toilets, to check my make-up and hair were up to scratch before facing the world.

11.10 a.m. Morning break: again, it was likely I would 'go to the toilet' and check my make-up and hair. I would frantically search for my make-up from my school bag before carefully updating my face until I was content. It's likely I would also mutter some negative words to myself about what I thought I looked like.

1.15 p.m. Before afternoon lessons were to commence, I would make sure to catch a glimpse of myself in the mirror or in the reflection of a window. Yup, you guessed it – I would top up my face or re-adjust my hair.

PS: On a normal day, even if I only went to Tesco, I would have to wear make-up.

Exhausted yet?!

I don't know about you, but seeing all of that written down on paper makes it seem SO SILLY. Yet it felt so normal and ordinary.

It was as if my life-project was to be pretty. Or beautiful. But pretty would suffice.

The big, bad problem

Comparison is one of the biggest issues we have with our bodies. It means that we look at the girl next door (not necessarily literally) and think that she's perfect and that if we looked like her then we would be 'sorted'. We see her perfection which somehow highlights our own imperfection.

Since I started Belle in 2015, I have had many questions and statements thrown my way casting doubt over my ability to lead Belle based on my appearance. For example, on the Tube a few months ago I started a conversation with a fellow passenger (I know, doesn't happen often, right?!). We shared life stories and of course I shared about Belle and the work I do with young women in schools. One thing she said struck me massively. She responded in disbelief, totally unconvinced that I could do what I do when I look the way I do. The only way I figured what she meant by me 'looking the way I do' was when she made hand signals to suggest that, in her mind, I am 'too pretty' to be doing the work I do; her issue was with my face and my body.

Ouch, how would I respond?

1 Don't judge a book by its cover (even though you probably judged this book by its cover!)
We look and then we judge and then we assume. I've struggled so much with the way I look over the years and I've

put so much of my value in it. I've looked in the mirror and only seen 'ugly' and 'not good enough'. Why do some people assume I haven't? We often have someone in our lives who we look at as 'perfect' and having it all together.

Why do we look at people and assume they have it all sussed? Why do we think that another woman's beauty disqualifies our own? And what if you're that 'perfect' girl to someone else?

2 Comparison is the thief of joy
We live in an image-saturated culture. I used to struggle even more with subconsciously comparing myself to other girls, whether in magazines, on TV or at school. No matter what we look like, comparison floods our lives.

Why do we sacrifice originality for competition?

3 Socially constructed ideas of beauty
What is considered 'beautiful' varies unbelievably between cultures and throughout time. It's constantly changing. If we 'attain' one thing, there's always more. We never reach the perfect, socially constructed idea of 'beauty'. If I strive for slimmer legs, I may attain them but then there'll be something more to chase after: a smaller waist, whiter teeth, a flatter stomach.

How can we live like this?

Don't compare your backstage to someone else's edited, filtered highlight reel

The way society does things

A word to sum up the way society does things is 'culture'. Culture plays a massive role in dictating what society deems 'beautiful'. Over recent years there has been a mega cultural shift which women of different ages have led across the world. Women are making a stand for what is true and what has been so drastically overlooked.

In a nutshell, 'beautiful' has always been what society deems to be 'beautiful'. To unpack this thought, imagine this sticker is stuck to your mirror:

> **You weren't born disliking your face or your body, you learned it from society at some point along the way, so now is the time to unlearn it and love your body.**

I think back to the sixteenth century when European women were expected to wear corsets and to change their form as what was considered fashionable changed. Read that again: they literally changed their body form to stay up to date with fashions. I did some research about corset controversy and found some articles entitled 'The slaves of fashion'. Some women wore corsets so tight that it restricted movement of the upper body. I reckon we do this in so many different ways today. To be a slave to something is to be forced to obey something. That may sound too strong but actually I think most of the time we don't feel we have a choice. The subtlety of 'beauty' in society doesn't undermine the power of it. We're slaves to the trends. We're slaves to our bodies. We're constantly finding fault with ourselves and striving and striving to stay fashionable and/or slim because we believe that genuine contentment will come from that . . . agreed? I know, I've been there!

OK, true, I've just chatted about beauty from a few hundred years ago. But even today we see trends in lip-fillers and body contouring. And even today we see such diversity in beauty standards around the world. If we want to strive and strive for beauty then we're constantly going to be let down. The standard of beauty is totally different across different cultures and different times. Let's look at the vast differentiation in beauty ideals across the world today. Of course, these are only generalizations proposed by the media:

Western: (we know this one well) the standard is to be tall and slender but busty.
French: the standard is to be refreshingly *au naturel*.
Korean: the standard is the perfection of complexion: porcelain skin is the ideal.
Indian: the standard is having thick, lustrous hair.
South American: the standard is a muscular and thicker bottom half.
Burmese: the standard is long necks.
Kenyan: the standard is long earlobes and shaved heads.

Anyhow . . . you get me? We literally cannot compare.

The power of media

Part of how society shapes what it is to be 'beautiful' is through advertising, which is essentially the way companies want you to think things are done. Check out these slogans:

'Are you beach body ready?' – by The Weightloss Collection.
'Save the whales: lose the blubber; go vegetarian' – by PETA.
'Love. Without the Handles' – by Popchips.
'The Perfect Body' – by Victoria's Secret.

As I said earlier, women have been speaking out about the horrors that they are being subjected to by the media, especially advertising. The problem is that so often we accept adverts for what they are and what they say, without challenging them and questioning how they affect us. For example, 'Are you beach body ready?' caused uproar when displayed on the hoardings of the London underground. Dove responded with the campaign, 'Every body's beach body ready'. Genius. And it's true.

Another subtle way that the media informs 'beauty' is by the women it gives airtime. For example, the women that are picked for adverts, the women chosen to be on the TV screen and the girls steeped in popularity on social media. Thankfully, this is changing. But often it was the following: slim, tall, white, beaming, a perfect complexion, shiny hair, long legs. I wonder what image comes to mind for you? This is not a fair representation of the girls on the planet. It doesn't represent me and it may not represent you.

The next time you see an advert, challenge the authority that it has over you.

The relationship that we humans have with our bodies is usually complex and negative. I think back to the film *Mean Girls* and the mirror scene where Regina and her crew are doing 'girl stuff' by chilling in her bedroom and chatting. They look in the mirror and start complaining about their appearance: their hips are too big, their shoulders are too wide, their hairline isn't right.

Now, *Mean Girls* isn't the best illustration for most things. BUT this interaction gives us a little insight into the brain of the girl and the weird comparison we set up between our bodies. We naturally try to find our faults and our imperfections and we find ourselves consumed by them.

This narrative needs to change. If we want to be women who stand strong, who love who they were created to be and who tell the story that they are more than their image, then we need to change the attitude we have towards our body. We need to change our perspective and our thoughts.

While I've been mainly focusing on girls, the relationship that boys have with their bodies is just as complex and negative. From countless conversations that I've had with them, I've been shocked by what I'll call their 'muscle insecurity'. You know all those magazines that we drool over with men displayed as eight-packed hunks? Well, when they don't measure up to that image of perfection, they experience insecurity too (and sometimes deal with it differently from us girls).

What you need to know about your body

- ☆ It's always ready to be in a bikini.
- ☆ Your body is not against you.

- ☆ What you want it to be should never be dictated by other people.
- ☆ Your body is beautiful in any shape.
- ☆ You will never reach the perfect body.
- ☆ Don't let your thoughts bully your body.
- ☆ The problem isn't your body, it's what you think of it.
- ☆ Beauty isn't determined by perfection, imperfection is beautiful.
- ☆ Healthy looks different on everyone.
- ☆ Boys also struggle with body image, not just girls.
- ☆ Loving your body is the greatest revolution.
- ☆ Your body is good regardless of what it looks like.

When it comes to starting the process of loving our bodies, we have to start with the tool that reflects our image: THE MIRROR. Dun. Dun. Dunnnnn (I hear you say). But seriously, the relationship we have with our mirror, and the words we speak to ourselves as we process the image in front of us, IS VITAL.

The other day I came across this beautifully written poem by the young Australian author Erin Hanson:

> Never trust a mirror,
> For a mirror always lies,
> It makes you think that all you're worth,
> Can never be seen from the outside.
> Never trust a mirror,
> It only shows you what's skin deep,
> You can't see how your eyelids flutter,
> When you're drifting off to sleep,

Your body is
FOR you, it's not
AGAINST you

It doesn't show you what the world sees,
When you're only being you,
Or how your eyes just light up,
When you're loving what you do,
It doesn't capture when you're smiling,
Where no-one else can see,
And your reflection cannot tell you,
Everything you mean to me,
Never trust a mirror,
For it only shows your skin,
And if you think that it dictates your worth,
It's time you looked within.

Read it again.

Take every word in.

Women and girls are coming together all over the globe to celebrate one another for the beauty of their inner selves. There is so much more to you than what meets the eye. And that is the most exciting thing EVER.

Tips and tricks

- ☆ Stop yourself before you say anything negative about your body (whether it's thoughts or words).
- ☆ If your friends start to criticize their own bodies, stop them and encourage them instead.
- ☆ Look in your mirror every morning and say to yourself, 'I am a girl, loved, treasured, adored and beautiful because I am who I am.'

AM I A SELFIE QUEEN?

A few years ago I started to explore why I was so obsessed with what I looked like. I started to chat with people (those my age and younger), to send out questionnaires and to read lots. One prominent voice for believing such things about myself was the voice of social media, in particular Instagram.

Now let me say, I am no granny or anything. I love social media (not that all grannies don't love social media . . .). I love its power to unite and connect people. I love the power it has to share a message and to encourage. Guess what: it barely existed when I was at school and it's more prominent now than it has ever been, along with other social media platforms which are constantly being created.

Social media is shaping our identity more than ever. It's also radically shaping the way we view our image.

Insta

Instagram, as we all know it, is a platform for capturing images, sharing videos and creating stories while following, engaging with and liking others' images and videos.

According to Instagram itself, it is 'a community of more than 300 million who capture and share the world's moments'.[3] Apparently, users share more than 60 million photos every day. So a very large proportion of human beings who walk the entire planet have Instagram. Most likely, the entire population of your school use Instagram. It's everywhere.

The extent to which Instagram is used is also mega (my personal research found that most teenage girls are using it constantly throughout the day). I can't begin to count the amount of times I have found myself caught in the trap of sitting and scrolling repeatedly down my feed, accidentally finding myself on the Instagram page of a friend's friend's friend. It's almost like an entire alternative universe and reality!

One minute I'll feel a random desire to find a quirky local coffee shop for an artisan latte. The next minute I'll find myself doing some online shopping after the inspiration of Insta (I say 'inspiration' but the likelihood is that I love someone's outfit so much that I feel the desire to scour the internet to find an exact replica . . .).

And maybe a few minutes later I'll be frantically doing sit-ups and squats, keeping my eyes peeled for that perfect thigh gap and toned stomach. Yikes, right?!?

One day, I took over the Instagram story for 40acts, a charity-led generosity challenge which runs every day of Lent in order to have an impact on people and their community.[4] The aim was to inspire many hundreds of people to be generous with their words. It was a lot of fun and super creative, but one thing I did note was just how flipping exhausted I was by the end of the day. The amount of energy, thought and time that went into creating the perfect (actually, not even near-perfect) story felt so unnatural! There would be moments where I'd shout, 'Wait, wait, do it again – I missed it!!!' And moments when we would work to carefully fabricate a moment to perfection. The reality is that it was pretty unreal, unnatural and unrepresentative of real life.

So last year I decided to take matters into my own hands and conducted some research with my Belle followers on social media. I decided that enough was enough. The thoughts that spiralled through my mind needed to be explored more objectively. I didn't want them to be based just on my opinions, but to be grounded in the thoughts and experiences of other girls.

From the 200 respondents, I found out the following things:

We use Instagram to share our lives with others

Thirty-seven per cent of teenage girls mainly use Instagram 'to show other people what I have/do'
This one we're probably all guilty of at different points in life. For example:

1. You invested in the most sexy outfit for a night out and must present what you look like to the world or it would be a wasted outfit.
2. You're on holiday and you must take photos to update people on your tanning situation in order to implicitly create jealously.

3 You climb to the top of a hill and take a picture to show the world what you did, but in reality you only climbed the hill in order to take the picture because you knew it'd get a whole loada likes.

OK, they might be extreme examples but they aren't that far off reality.

PS: please do take pictures on a night out, on holiday and if you climb hills for a living: capturing memories and moments is one of life's most special things.

I'm going on about this because (remember what I always say) awareness = action. We have to be aware of the impact of the big influences in our lives and social media is a mega-influencer. Keep reading and it will become clear as we go along!

We use Instagram to follow other people's lives

Seventy-eight per cent of teenage girls mainly use Instagram 'to see what other people are doing'

I found this to be pretty bizarre, to be honest! Do you not think that sounds a bit nosy and boring? I know that in reality it isn't boring but seeing it written down makes it sound a bit (*correction* 'very') lame . . .

Thirty-seven per cent of teenage girls mainly use Instagram 'to follow celebs and those Instafamous'

FYI: by 'Instafamous' I mean the people with thousands upon thousands of followers, likes and comments. They are also the Instagrammers who are paid by brands to post images/

videos/stories using/wearing/holding their products as another form of advertising.

This means that a lot of the Instafamous fabricate their images to look more perfect than reality, to create more engagement with their post in order to make more money or gain more online popularity.

They post enticing images of adventure, beauty and inspiration. But this involves constant planning to make life look good on screen. One ex-Instagram model has a really inspiring story. Her name is Essena O'Neill. Her story of radical rejection of social media made national and international headlines. She was earning a living through posting perfected images on her Instagram feed and being paid by various companies to do so (i.e. some photos would be taken in various clothes as a means of advertising). In 2015 she went through her Instagram page and either deleted thousands of photos because of their sole purpose of self-promotion or re-edited the captions to reveal the manipulation and insecurities behind them. She realized she was unhealthily consumed by it, and opened up about her experience in videos, blog posts and interviews. Check out her story because it's a game-changer.

It's an all-consuming, exhausting and life-absorbing task to submit such pixilated perfection on screen. PLUS, it means we are constantly scrolling through some images which are not representative of real, real life. We get into a mode of thinking which assumes that everyone else is living such glamorous lives, and then there's us in the corner . . . it's hard to distinguish what represents reality.

Is Instagram good?

When I asked teenage girls about the influence Instagram has on them, *52 per cent* believed that Instagram has a positive effect on their self-esteem.

ARE YOU SHOCKED? I was shocked (!!!). I had totally assumed that Instagram was bad, bad, bad for our self-esteem, so why are people saying it's positive?! However, I understood this more when I read some of the heartbreaking reasons girls thought that Instagram was good for their self-esteem. I reckon that as a society we are baffled about the implications of Instagram for our self-esteem. Here are some of the things the girls said about Instagram:

'All I want is to look like them, be like them, do what they do, but I know I will never get to'

Forty-three per cent of the girls referred to Instagram making them compare themselves with others. This is scaaaaaaaary because of its inaccurate representation of someone's life. Instagram promotes pixilated perfection. Our thoughts about the lives of others are distorted, which means that our thoughts about the value of our own lives are distorted. We compare our true reality with other people's edited reality.

'If I don't get likes I know the picture is ugly so I just delete it'

Ahhhhhhhhhh, this makes me so sad!!! Plus, some others said their happiness depends on the amount of likes they get. Despite some understanding about the fake element to social media, teenage girls are still stressing to gain likes, comments and followers – meaning they delete the posts that don't live up to expectation. We CANNOT use Instagram to find a version of ourselves that receives the most positive social engagement. We will be so unhappy.

'People put comments saying that you are not worth living and it takes a toll on your self-confidence'
This is absolutely heartbreaking. Instagram allows us to be pretty anonymous: we don't necessarily know who everyone is on our feed and we can comment what we like, when we like. We can write stuff online whether it's valid or not valid, whether it's true or false. The views of other people affect the way we view ourselves when they should NOT.

'Because you can post good selfies and feel great and get lots of likes and it makes me feel like everyone likes me'
Although we can use the social network to build and encourage one another, there is a fine line between receiving this out of love and obsessing over receiving it in order to justify our existence. Our thoughts about our image cannot rest on the opinion of Instagrammers.

What's the point?

Although the majority of teenage girls thought Instagram has a great impact on their self-esteem, in most cases it totally does not. We have to be so careful. Who we are is not what we look like. Who we are is not what other people say we are. Who we are is not the amount of likes we get on a photo.

Tips and tricks

- ☆ Try and last one week without Instagram and see how your mood changes.
- ☆ Unfollow anyone whose posts are unhealthy and damaging for your self-esteem.

BE BEAUTIFUL

This is the point at which we must reassess all that has been said through the lens of this:

> **For you are God's MASTERPIECE, created anew in Christ Jesus to do the good things he planned for you long ago.**
>
> **(Ephesians 2.10)**

The *Mona Lisa* is a great example of a worldly masterpiece. It's renowned, it's well known and it's adored. It's also apparently worth around £15 million (although it's difficult to track down the cost of it!). Now, I am no incredible artist. So, imagine if I were to try and recreate the *Mona Lisa* and pop it on eBay to sell it . . . how much do you reckon it would go for? Weird question, right?! It probably wouldn't sell for anything – it probably wouldn't sell at all. I use this as an illustration because someone once said to me, 'An original is worth more than a copy.' The point is not that we put a price on ourselves and on other people, but that we focus on the fact that we are each original masterpieces! Our focus and our attention should not be on comparison and copying. Our focus should be on believing that we are

What people say is a

reflection of them,

not of you

masterpieces and moving forward BOLDLY, assured of our value and beauty.

It's tricky though, right?!

So, let's go back over 'beauty' while seeing ourselves as a masterpiece.

Am I enough?

The problem with our culture of celebrating princesses and dolls is that we are celebrating the illusion of perfection. What I mean is that these toys we play with become the image in our mind of perfect femininity (or even just femininity) to strive for. They inherently make us feel inadequate.

The world says we aren't smart enough, pretty enough, thin enough, rich enough. Yet the world says we're too loud or we're too insecure. It's a paradox of our perceived insignificance.

We always want to be 'prettier', 'smarter', 'thinner' and the danger of these words is the 'er' part. We'll always believe that we aren't enough if we aren't satisfied with where we are NOW.

What if we were to wake up every morning believing that we are going to be the best version of ourselves, rather than seeing ourselves as a work in progress? I wonder how that would change our mindset and perspective?! IT EXCITES ME.

Imagine how much more confidence we would have to do so many more things.

God chose us before the creation of the world (Ephesians 1.4). He is the greatest artist of all time. He's infinitely creative and we are his.

You know when you go shopping and you see your favourite brand with a new 'limited edition' item (whether it's a make-up palette, knitted jumper or candle [yes I love candles]). Those items are one-offs, custom-made, extremely valuable and high in demand. Well, when God made you, he made you to be a limited edition; he custom-made each and every one of us. Sounds familiar to the idea of a masterpiece, doesn't it? We are not 'too this' or 'too that'. We are enough. But we have to believe that we are enough.

When God looks at us he knows our failures and our mistakes, but he's a God who still sees us and says, 'My beautiful child.'

He says:

> You are enough because of who you are and I created you exactly that way. Don't waste time being side-tracked by looks: they will only fade over time and they won't fill that empty void within you. You'll never have enough of the worldly things because there are so many distractions and temptations, and they won't satisfy you anyway. But be secure in knowing that I am enough for you. I will not let you down. You can trust my love.

Am I pretty?

With regards to faith, I have battled this question for a long while. Initially, I would've never turned to look at what the Bible says about beauty and attractiveness, but my journey of faith has only ignited my passion to live a godly life as a godly woman. So when I finally turned to the Bible to see what God said about our striving to be 'pretty', I have to be honest with my findings!! It's a touchy one and you are so welcome to disagree. BUT first give it a read, dig into your own Bible, discuss with your mates and then come to your own conclusion. Here goes . . .

I found out that concerning ourselves with being pretty is NOT biblical.

When I first heard that, I was pretty miffed. I thought the following thoughts:

'If I'm not striving to be pretty then what am I striving for?'
'What if feeling pretty feels like enough?'
'Why did God create people who look so different?'
'I kinda assumed my purpose as a girl and as a woman was and is to be pretty.'

You may read those and think I WAS SO VAIN and you may well be right.

On the other hand, when I found out that concerning ourselves with being pretty isn't biblical, I WAS SO RELIEVED. The pressure lifted. My heart shifted. I felt the desire to dream bigger. It sounds so silly, but when we're so wrapped up in our image we become obsessed by it and turn away from our purpose and passion.

Before I get too carried away, let's have a look at some actual Bible verses:

'You are God's masterpiece' (Ephesians 2.10) We all know this one from the whole premise of the book. All masterpieces are different, right? Some are weird and some are obscure; they're still masterpieces as they are. Wearing more make-up, owning more fashionable clothes and becoming slimmer won't change the fact that you are already a masterpiece of God's. Ultimately, you are God's.

'So do not worry, saying . . . "What shall we wear?"' (Matthew 6.31) Jesus is saying, 'Hey girl, it doesn't matter what you wear! There are so many more important things to focus on. Don't get side-tracked by something so insignificant.' I don't think I need to say any more to summarize this one!

'Your beauty should not come from outward adornment, such as elaborate hairstyles and the wearing of gold jewellery or fine clothes. Rather, it should be that of your inner self' (1 Peter 3.3–4) This kind of suggests that beauty is an inward attitude, right? So, what if working on our inner beauty were our life-project, rather than our outer beauty? This verse isn't saying that we have to go about life being quiet and fading into the background, but what I think it means is that inward beauty is the important kind that radiates more spectacularly than any other.

As I've grown up I've become more confident in the beauty of my inner life, my personality. I've also grown in the understanding that beauty radiates from the kind and gentle spirit that God has entrusted me with. I believe that, for me, this has made me more approachable and allowed God to speak through me in more spectacular ways because it's so unexpected that I would (a) be able to speak at conferences/events/church and (b) be able to write a book.

So, when we realign ourselves with the biblical truth about beauty, we see that God-confidence is the key to self-confidence, which allows us to radiate beauty to those around us (in what we say, do and believe) instead of being enslaved by the expectations of the beauty industry.

The thing is that God doesn't see our struggle with our appearance and dismiss it. He is a totally caring God. He sees our struggle and *he longs for us to be free from it*. The image that comes to mind is that of a caterpillar being contained by its cocoon and longing to be free to spread its wings as a beautiful butterfly. He longs for us to be free from what traps and confines us. He wants you to be free to know and love who you are.

Am I a selfie queen?

On our quest to be free to love ourselves as God created us to be, one of the things that can be trapping is social media.

When it comes to social media, Instagram in particular, being free from other people's opinions with regards to appearance is LIFE-changing – it's a pretty big deal.

When we live in freedom, we live in God's master-story, embracing his masterpiece for our lives. It also starts a journey of us looking at other people and embracing the fact that they too are a masterpiece. They might not know that and they might not feel that way but it's exactly how God sees them. You may not feel that way about them either. It may sometimes feel like they don't deserve it. But it's likely that neither do we.

Living in freedom is about letting go of who we're supposed to be and embracing who we really are.

What do we need to let go of?

I've made a list:

1. What other people comment online
2. What other people 'like' or don't 'like' online
3. What other people post online.

Notice that every single one starts with what 'other people' do or say. When it comes to social media, our focus seems to be on other people (but in a negative way). We get totally engrossed in their lives, their opinions, their posts, their likes. We need to let go of those things. We need to move away from comparison towards inspiration, where we can be encouraged by what we see, without having it negatively affect our own sense of self.

When we let go of things, we need to take hold of new things – new ways of thinking and being. I came across the following verse in the Bible:

> **God pays no attention to what others say (or what you think) about you. He makes up his own mind.**
>
> **(Romans 2.11, *The Message*)**

HOW FREEING IS THAT? To know what God's mind says about who we are requires time spent in his presence, listening to him and reading his Word.

In a society that profits from our self-doubt, insecurity and anxiety, loving who we truly are is a rebellious act.

Can you remember who you were before the world told you who you should be?

In a society that encourages competition between girls, believing that other girls are masterpieces is revolutionary.

Social media and self-image don't express reality. The reality of who we are is who God created us to be.

We need no permission to be who we are: only courage to escape the cage that confines us and stretch our wings and

The *reality* of who we *are* is who God *created* us to be

fly. We find freedom when we find God because, as John 8.32 says:

> **If you stick with this, living out what I tell you, you are my disciples for sure. Then you will experience for yourselves the truth, and the truth will free you.**
>
> **(*The Message*)**

Be free from expectation, pressure and perfection, and in doing so you will become beautiful: a beauty full of faith, truth and freedom.

PURPOSE

AM I WHAT HAS HAPPENED TO ME?

I wonder what your most significant life event is.
I wonder what has happened to you.
I wonder what monumental experiences you've had.

You know the cliché 'Life is a rollercoaster': well, it's pretty flipping true, girls! There will be times when we don't feel OK and times when bad things happen. I wish I could tell you otherwise! There are, of course, such great things that we get to experience and accomplishments we can celebrate too.

Another well-known saying is 'Life is an adventure', and anyone who knows me well knows that it's one of my life-sayings!! By 'life-sayings' I mean it's one of those sayings that gets me through a lot of things; it re-orientates me and brings perspective.

For example, when bad stuff happens, my thoughts go something like this: 'You know what, life isn't boring, it's an adventure, which means there will be ups and downs but I won't be in this down place for too long, I need to be courageous and keeping moving forward, living expectantly for the next "up" moment', rather than 'my life sucks, it's useless and I'm useless'.

AND when great stuff happens (like being offered a contract to write this book!), my thoughts go a little like this: 'Life is so flipping cool, I love this adventure that I'm living and I love how unique it is to me, I'm so grateful for all of life's surprises and celebrations.'

Life is a matter of choices

One thing you may notice about my little Jessie-thoughts illustration is the element of choice that is displayed. What I mean by this is the fact that I could choose how to respond to whatever happened in my life (and continually try to do so today). I could choose to flip out or I could choose to find the gold in the rubbish.

What I also think is vital is separating what happens to us and who we are. We are not what we experience. We are not what happens to us. Yes, we are a product of these things, but we have the power of choice over how we interpret our experiences (good and bad). Failing at something doesn't make you a failure. You may have noticed one of my lines of thought is 'It's useless, I'm useless': this is the kind of thing I'm talking about. You are what you choose to become. You are how you choose to react. You are what your mind interprets you to be.

At this point, let me say that I haven't always been able to think this way. And to this day, I don't always succeed in trying.

One of the pivotal moments in my life that stands out because of the hurt and pain I endured takes us all the way back to my birthday party the summer before year 9. You've already read what my experience was back then. Because of what happened, my mind unravelled into self-hatred and I was fed up with being me. Looking back, however, I know that I had a role to play. If I hadn't been so focused on the wrong things, I wouldn't have found myself in the position that I was in. I look back and see the victim-mentality that overtook my whole being and outlook. Victims view themselves through the filter of: 'It's not my fault, it happened to me, life is too difficult, they did it to me, everyone always does stuff to me.' Do you get the gist a little?

The problem with this mentality is that we stop looking for a solution to the problem because we feel like nothing can be done. We also have the tendency to over-focus on ourselves and how we are the victim. Don't worry, this is pretty normal behaviour. But this is also where it comes back to the power of choice we have over our thoughts, behaviour, feelings and actions. The most exciting thing is to move from 'It happened to me' to 'I'm going to make the best of this situation.' It not only changes our perspective on life but it changes what other people see when they look at us: it has the power to inspire and transform rather than enslave and victimize! My experience of bullying and self-hatred has given me a passion and a desire to journey with girls who experience a similar thing and feel a similar way. I'm grateful that I can empathize with how they feel. It has taken years to get to this point, but nonetheless I am thankful.

When I think of people who have shown this ability to inspire and transform themselves through a perspective shift, I think of female activist Malala Yousafzai. She was on the receiving end of death threats, danger and bullets because of her campaign for the right to education, yet she was resilient. Malala was not confined by what happened to her, but has thrived in her quest for a solution. She was the co-recipient of the 2014 Nobel Peace Prize and, in 2017, started her education at Oxford University. Wow.

One final note for you:

Don't do it alone.

Don't face whatever the mountain is in front of you by yourself. We were created to live in community with one another. We were created to lean on each other in tough times. Sometimes we find ourselves in a rut. That's OK. Sometimes what we face is absolutely gigantic and absolutely terrifying. Don't fret. Surround yourselves with people who know and love you.

Life is to be lived adventurously. And adventure is in the journey of life, not the destination. Embrace the journey despite the setbacks, knowing that there is joy and beauty in the little things along the way!

Tips and tricks

- ☆ Choose three people who you know you can count on to tell them how you're feeling.
- ☆ Is your mindset 'life is an adventure' or 'life is rubbish to me'? Does it need to shift?

I don't want to be remembered as the GIRL who was SHOT,
I want to be remembered as the GIRL who STOOD UP

Malala Yousafzai

AM I HAPPY?

'Am I happy?' has to be one of the most complicated questions we ever ask. So many of us reject the idea of being happy for a ton of reasons about why we couldn't, shouldn't and mustn't be happy. Life is no walk in the park. Shock, horror, right?! Nah. We all know that for sure. But I want to use this chapter to explore some coping mechanisms and unravel this meaning of 'happiness' a tad with the aim of enabling us to live in all fullness, adventure and contentment.

What is happiness anyway?

Happiness. I wonder what it means to you. Think of the word association game and ponder what words come to mind for you. It might be 'fun', 'laughter', 'love', 'holidays', 'freedom', 'pizza', 'chocolate', 'cake' (or 'chocolate cake', actually) . . . wow, that escalated quickly! I do legit have a serious point to make!

It's a pretty elusive word itself, not anything we usually give that much thought to! When I look back I know I spent a significant amount of life living for weekends and holidays (TGIF and all that). I impatiently awaited lying flat out on a sunbed by a pool and soaking up the rays of sunshine that are totally impossible to rely on in the UK. But girls, I'm so quickly learning that happiness isn't to be awaited, it's to be embedded into our life. It is NOT reliant on future things such as when you have a boyfriend, when you're slimmer, when you earn more money or when you go to university. Make a choice to be happy in your circumstances NOW.

Make little choices on a daily basis. It's achievable; it's not far away.

So what am I on about . . . what are these little choices?! Not long ago I sat pondering what the little things are in life that bring me happiness. I like to think I'm brave enough to share my list with you now (if you promise not to take the mick . . .):

- ☆ A large mug of green tea
- ☆ Listening to worship music
- ☆ Bringing my breakfast to bed and reading in bed
- ☆ Laughing with friends
- ☆ New adventures in new places
- ☆ Cooking meals
- ☆ Looking after small children
- ☆ Taking a short stroll outdoors.

These are such mediocre, normal, little things – yes, I totally agree! But they are monumental in creating present happiness rather than seeking a future, far-off happiness.

Now, believe me, I know some of you reading this will be so far from happy that you pretty much want to skip this section. Please don't. You may feel like the reasons are so big that no little change or little choice will change it. I know I'm no expert in the matter, but my prayer and hope is that sharing some of my story, failures and successes will inspire you by offering hope, understanding and help!

I also realize that the state of our world is a little confusing, baffling and, more than that, heartbreaking. So my focus will remain on us as individuals and how we can be equipped to shine so brightly within ourselves that the light is contagious to all those around us. Bring it on, right?!

So what squashes our capacity for happiness?

Worry is wild

Worry is a big'un. Worry is a sinking feeling. Worry is uncertainty about potential problems, troubles or fears. Worry is something faced by every human on the planet, no matter how 'sorted' their life may seem from the outset. Let that be an encouragement to you that it's OK to feel this way. Worry just needs to be tamed.

I'm sure you can think of scenarios where you have worried so much about a particular situation that you've lost sleep over it, you've lost mental space as it's swirled around and around endlessly in your mind and it has subsequently arrested your sense of happiness, life and joy. I've experienced that COUNTLESS times. Yet, when the situation/day/time arises, it's never as bad as it once seemed and my inner monologue promises myself that I won't let it happen again.

Worry is like an elusive emotion arising inconveniently and self-destructively.

Rationalizing is a pretty great antidote to worry. I've pondered this for a while and will explain exactly what I mean by it. I am so grateful for the close relationship I have with my mum. She is an absolute wonder-woman (I'd share her if I could). Whenever I would feel worried about an event, situation, exam, relationship (or anything, for that matter), I knew I could share it with her. Her wisdom would often take the form of a question, such as: 'What's the worst that could happen?' Often the worst thing that could happen would sound so dramatic, petty or unlikely (i.e. worry about exams when the worst-case scenario would be a bad grade, and life is so much bigger than that) that it would release me from the worry itself. It sounds simple and totally useless but it has the power to transform mindsets and release us from the captivity of worry. It opens us up to the realization that actually the worst-case scenario is not so paralysing after all.

At this point, I want to mention that there are very real worries that we face in life. These may be worries about illness, money, family or death, for example. No one can tell you that what you're feeling is invalid. If this is the case and this is something you are facing, I am with you in this. I may not know you and I won't know about your situation but, believe me, you are not alone. There is a sisterhood of women across the world who are right behind you and are cheering you on. May I suggest confiding in someone that you trust to talk through these feelings of real worry? A problem shared is a problem halved (so the saying goes).

Corrie ten Boom was an amazing young girl who took on the courageous role of hiding Jews throughout the Second World War. She is a legend. She saved lives. She lived on the edge of losing her life through what she chose to do. Why is this relevant? Because this is one of the things she writes in her book *The Hiding Place*: 'Worry does not empty tomorrow of its sorrow, it empties today of its strength.' Flip right? What an incredible young woman. She lived every day for what it was and faced what it brought with the assurance that she could conquer it, and would do the same when the tomorrow came.

Worry only has power when we let it. When we rationalize, we announce that worry is no longer welcome in our heads and our hearts. Give it a go.

Anxiety is all-consuming

I want to take a little pause to talk about anxiety. At the time of confirming that I would be writing this book, I had never once experienced such a thing as anxiety. A few years ago I had heard people talk about it and read a few articles concerning it but hadn't fully understood it until I experienced it. It's a major concern for us in the world we live in, with a quarter of young women in the UK suffering from anxiety and depression.[5] Anxiety is also a rising concern in young people contacting Childline.[6]

A couple of years ago, my family and I went on an adventure-filled trip to South Africa and Mauritius for a couple of weeks. Yes, it was incredible, beautiful, stunning, and the Instagrams were top notch. But what social media didn't show, and what I have never shared publicly or even with very many people at all, is that I had an anxiety-fuelled panic attack during one of the nights of our stay in Cape Town. I had heard of the phrase 'panic attack' before but had just assumed that rationale and logic would steer someone clear of such an experience – naive, I know.

I'd experienced waves of anxiety throughout our trip so far, not being sure what the cause of them was nor how to make them subside. I was always known as the logical child in our family who would analyse cause and effect, keep the peace in arguments and strive to ensure happiness for all. When waves of anxiety rush through your body, it's the most frustrating thing to not be able to trace them back to an anxiety-causing event. My anxious waves culminated one evening. My sister and I were getting ready for bed. I was fine. I brushed my teeth, washed my face and slipped on my pyjamas as I always did. I pulled back the covers of the double bed I would be sharing with my sister that night and curled up with my duvet pulled up high and head sunk into the pillow. I checked through my phone one last time and announced a 'Goodnight, mate' to my sister, who was lying next to me.

What I can only estimate as being the next half-hour or so was rife with emotional turbulence. Anxious thoughts were rushing through my head and my body. I was frustrated with the inability to shake it off, thinking that it was silly, avoidable and pointless. I attempted to logically weave my way out of the cocoon that was trapping me inside myself. My heart rate began to quicken so I began to count sheep, count to ten, take deep breaths – anything! Within minutes I had lost all control, and my pulse beat faster than I thought humanly possible as panic arose from the depths of my soul, or at least the depths of somewhere, though I didn't know where.

The only thing running through my head was the realization that this was a panic attack, that I now understood how terrifying and crippling they are and that I didn't know how to make it stop.

I didn't dare wake up my sister.

Soon, my heart rate began to slow down and somehow total exhaustion sent me to sleep. The next morning I felt too embarrassed and ashamed to explain to my family that I thought I'd had a panic attack during the night. I texted a friend who I knew would understand and she clarified that, yes, it was indeed. I sat at the breakfast table and burst into tears; my heart rate was increasing again and I had no idea how to make it stop.

So there you have it. It was exhausting. I haven't had another one to date – not yet. And a part of me is glad to be able to identify with what it is and what it feels like. I now understand just a tiny part of what some people have to battle on a daily basis. And for that I am actually thankful.

As I explained, I definitely like to think about things logically!! One of the worries I had is that the anxiety was caused by not having had enough rest and overworking my mind, body and soul. Being away meant that I was needing to readjust to a new routine and new places, and I just don't think I could hack it! What I've tried to take from this experience is that *rest is central to our wellbeing*. Biblically, we know the purpose of the Sabbath is to include rest in the rhythm of life. Apparently, some of the world's geniuses, including Darwin and Einstein, rested in between spouts of creative inspiration![7]

Society is moving so fast that it's exhausting even thinking about trying to keep up with it. Often we'll be tempted to put our work in front of our wellbeing, so we'll work 50-hour weeks and sacrifice our sleep and our health, but this doesn't allow our mind, body or soul to have some TLC. You may think I sound like an old woman right now (no offence to old women out there, you're super-wise and I long to be like you!!) but take a look at my examples below to see how relevant and do-able it is to REST:

Comfy-ify I realize this is not a word but I just quite like it, so bear with me!! The Danish word *hygge* was shortlisted as the *Oxford English Dictionary*'s Word of the Year in 2016 (good luck pronouncing it!). It refers to a feeling and a lifestyle. It's about making the little, simple and small things special and extraordinary. For me, highlighting the power in the little, simple and small things takes our mind away from the large, anxiety-provoking things in life. Hygge could be lighting a candle and cosying up with a blanket. It could be taking the time to enjoy every sip of your tea.

Sleep I know – it's not the most exciting example, is it, really!! My housemates and I joke all the time about the fact that 10.00–10.30 seems to have become our 'house bedtime'! We love our sleep. We know how much it affects our approach to the next day: whether we're too exhausted to function or buzzing for what's ahead. When my body is rested, my mind and soul awake feeling refreshed and reset for the day ahead. Sometimes I may sound and look silly getting an early night but, frankly, I know myself and I know I'm way more pleasant company having had my sleep!

Energizers This one is super fun. We aren't robots, plodding around getting tasks done. Basically, we were created to enjoy the adventure-filled life set out for us; to embrace possibility, challenge and thrill. We have to create time to do the things that bring us energy and spark life in the depths of our soul. Acknowledge what energizes you and make time for it (it doesn't have to require money). Be childlike in your approach too. My energizers are definitely going to the gym, finding a spot with a beautiful view or going out with friends. It may be getting your nails done, reading a good book or baking a delicious cake. Find time, guard the time and ENJOY.

Mindfulness Experiencing anxiety made me very aware of the relationship between my mind and body and the impact of one on the other. I realized I was abandoning my mind and letting it run a little wild. I wasn't tuned into my thoughts, worries and anxieties, which didn't allow me to refute and dismiss them. Mindfulness is about being aware. It's not some loopy, far-off thing. It's transformative, peace-bringing and powerful. It's about tuning into the thoughts that are running through our mind and acknowledging them without letting them consume us. An example might be: 'I recognize that I feel annoyed right now but that is a feeling and I will watch it pass, just as I stand by the side of the road and watch the traffic pass . . .' (Side note: if this intrigues you, I recommend you read up some more about it; Google is a genius.)

I'm no expert at mental health issues. But what I do know is that mental health is worthy of the same respect, care and affection as any physically visible illness or injury. I have so

Authenticity is about the choice to show up and be real. The choice to be honest. The choice to let our true selves be seen

Brené Brown

much admiration for people who have fought their corner and stood up for what is right and worthy of love.

And do you know what, it's OK not to be OK. It's OK to be vulnerable. It's OK to say how you're really feeling. It's OK to talk. It's OK to ask for help. There is no shame. There is power in your voice. There is power when you speak out.

Fear can be fierce

Fear is crippling. We all know the feeling arising from our stomach up to our throat. Fear can be rational and fear can be irrational. We know that fear can arise from the smallest of things, like the fear of missing a flight, or the largest of things, like coming face to face with a phobia (my mind is currently imagining snakes . . . not a phobia but I'm definitely not a fan). Fear can exist for a moment and fear can remain for what feels like or is literally a lifetime.

Fears manifest themselves in so many different ways. Fear of the unknown, fear of the future, fear of missing out, fear of change, fear of expectations, fear of death, fear of failure, fear of standing out, fear of fitting in are only a few examples of fear catching hold of us and not letting go.

I have to be honest at this point and say that, throughout my lifetime so far, I have steered clear of fear at any opportune moment. I lived safely. I liked routine. I avoided anything extraordinary. I embraced normality. Now, that's totally not to say that fear isn't experienced in normality, but I just never put myself out there!! But even this itself stemmed from a fear of failure. I never did anything radical, adventurous, life-giving, soul-feeding because I didn't want to do it badly, or fail or feel stupid and let myself down, or my family or friends or God. This was until I traded the option of comfortable student life studying in Southampton with an internship in Australia (as I mentioned earlier on). It went strongly against the persuading voice of my tutor telling me to study Business and French, and part of it went against myself and my desire for success, achievement and money (in the long term!).

Courage is the antidote to fear. I was helping at a kids' camp during my very first week in a place called Wollongong (just south of Sydney, if you like to imagine these things) and – three days in – was immediately confronted with the choice of whether or not to defeat Goliath. Goliath was a giant swing. Not only was it a giant swing but I was told it was the highest giant swing in the Southern Hemisphere. It involved being harnessed (never a pleasant feeling), putting on these half-goggle, half-glasses type things and being instructed that once you get to the top (hauled up by your friends pulling a rope tirelessly – a bit like a tug-of-war), you must, all by yourself and of your own accord, pull a lever that will release you and send you falling (or, more precisely, swinging) 26 metres. That's high. That's fear-inducing. I stood staring up at the giant, knowing I had a choice. I could say no or I could say yes.

I knew that if fear was just a feeling then an action could dissolve it. I knew that courage was not the absence of fear but required 'doing it anyway'. I knew that if I could be courageous with a seemingly small thing (though it was gigantic in size) then who knew what I could go on to defeat.

I said yes. My friends started pulling the rope. I started slowly ascending, metre by metre. My heart was in my stomach. People were cheering in their distinctly Aussie accents. I felt afraid. Metres went by in a flash. I reached the top. I attempted to admire the view during the petrifying few seconds I was at the top. The chanted countdown began.

Three! 'Oh pants, this is so high.'
Two! 'There's literally no other way to get down from here.'
One! 'I'm gonna have to pull the cord straight away or any hesitation will be disastrous.'
ZERO! 'This is terrifying . . .'

A few seconds of courage is all it takes to defeat a fear-inducing giant. It doesn't mean the fear doesn't exist but it does mean that you can overcome it. The cord is in your hands. The decision is in your head. The choice will affect your heart.

One inspirational woman who has written about courage is Brené Brown. In her book *The Gifts of Imperfection*, she reflects upon a totally revolutionary load of research for both psychology and Christianity. One of the things she says is this: 'Choosing courage does not mean that we're unafraid, it means that we are brave *enough* despite the fear and uncertainty.' Sometimes all it takes is mustering up enough bravery to face what's in front of us. It doesn't mean we appear all guns blazing, kitted out and riding into battle on a horse. Sometimes it's quiet small displays of bravery that overcome fear and uncertainty one step at a time.

Now girls, it's all been a little heavy reading, hasn't it? It's all a bit negative and it's all a bit 'blurghhhh'. Negative thinking is something we do need to explore because it's so prominent in girlhood. I don't know why, but it just tends to take centre-stage in our minds! I remember this vividly at school, and it doesn't subside as you get 'adulting' unless you address it. Whenever people said anything about me, I would immediately assess why they said what they said, what was in it for them and what they really meant (with a negative spin on it, of course!). Everything became a bit of a brain battle: a battle of distrust of others' thoughts and of my own thoughts. For example, if someone commented that I was being quiet (it's happened many times!!) then my thoughts would unravel as follows: 'If she said that it must be true', 'If she said that it must be a negative thing', 'She must think I'm quiet and lame and too introverted', 'How will I ever make friends if I'm so quiet?', 'How will I get through life being quiet?', 'I must become even quieter and retreat into my shell even more because that's evidently who I am and I feel weak' . . .

Everything was a distorted mosaic of distorted opinions. Whose opinion was I supposed to trust and believe?!

Some of the thoughts making up the mosaic of my mind were the following: 'I'm a failure', 'I'm not good enough', 'What's the point?', 'I'm unlovable', 'it's useless, I'm useless'.

Our thinking is strongly influential to our feeling and our feeling is strongly influential to our actions. According to

Google, we have around 150 thoughts a minute, so imagine the effect of the majority being negative!!

Henry David Thoreau, an American writer and political figure, says: 'Thought is the sculptor who can create the person you want to be.' That means that our thoughts shape our identity; they shape who we are and who we become. In this sense, they are active and alive. The more positive our thoughts are, the more positive we will feel about who we are.

So if thought is so crucial to our wellbeing, let's explore some mini little training methods for our mind: little ways to shift our mind and turn away from the negative rut we so readily find ourselves in and are attempting to dig our way out of.

Here are four ways to manage our thoughts (side note: I love the idea of 'managing our thoughts' because it gives authority, power and control back to us and makes us a key influencer, transformer and life-changer!):

1 Think of the big picture

This is all about zooming out of our situation or bubble and taking a look at it with fresh eyes. I'm a lover of panoramic, mountain-top (or hill-top, to be fair!) views – imagine it like that! Zooming out, taking a fresh look and embracing the view. This changes our perspective. It adds a new filter on our life-glasses.

If we start feeling negatively about a situation, it's helpful to gain perspective by pondering whether we'll still be negative, anxious or worried about it in, for example, four days' time, four weeks' time, four months' time, four years' time . . . It may sound drastic but it's vital to shifting our thoughts and crawling out of the negative cave that our mind can become.

I'll give you an example. At school I would become worried about certain exams – really worried, a life-consuming worry. Shifting my perspective to pondering about four months' time got me through the exam season. I would, instead, think the following: 'Hmm, once these exams are over, they're over and in four months' time they'll be over – and I desperately want to open my results and be proud of what I've achieved. So you know what, Jessie, work as hard as possible because you may as well, and know that the end is in sight. You won't be stuck here for ever so make the most of it.' Kind of get my gist? And also another insight into how my brain seems to work?!

2 Find the evidence

Is there actually anything to suggest that what you're thinking is true in any way? When we think that we're useless, we must become a detective. We need to explore whether there is any ounce of reality in our thoughts by examining the evidence.

This is because so often what we think about ourselves is not really what we think about ourselves; rather, it's what society has conditioned us to believe. Or we've let our mind run wild and think things waaaay beyond any element of truth.

In school I would go through periods of time feeling like an absolute failure. It was a recurring thought running laps around my brain. If I were to find the evidence to test whether this was true, I might find that I received a lower grade in my

English mock GCSE (this is true!). Now, a lower grade isn't actually a fail. Plus, it was the lowest grade I had ever received. So actually I was not failing, I was not a failure. It was one hiccup that just required a re-routing of my thoughts: 'I am not a failure, I am not failing. It's OK not to be good at everything and succeed 100 per cent of the time. This is a learning curve and I am OK with it. I am good enough as I am.'

3 Be compassionate with yourself

So often, one negative thought spirals out of control and we find ourselves having arrived at a mental destination that was never once intended for us. Don't overgeneralize. Don't let your thoughts have some crazy, out-of-control domino effect.

We talk about being compassionate in the way we treat other people, yet we struggle when it comes to being compassionate with ourselves. I'm sure many of us have had friends who have struggled with negative thoughts of some kind (whether about their appearance, ability or achievement) – would you respond to them how you talk to yourself? Would you affirm that, yes, they are useless, a failure, insignificant . . . ? I'd hope not. So why do we so easily talk to ourselves like that?

We must be self-compassionate in a way that embraces the fact that, yes, we are imperfect human beings but, YES, we are capable, we are desirable, we are worthy.

4 Find the one truth

Sometimes it's tricky to distinguish between what is a negative thought and what is, ultimately, a true and correct thought. I

Happiness is a state of **mind,**

and depends very little on

outward *circumstances*

Helen Keller

always struggled to make the distinction. We have to choose to believe the thoughts that are true about who we are: and our Creator is the one who knows us best.

Tips and tricks

- ☆ Try one of the methods of 'wellbeing' each day this week (comfy-ify, sleep, energizers or mindfulness).
- ☆ When a friend starts thinking and speaking negatively, try and coach her out of it using one of the four methods above.

AM I SIGNIFICANT?

Do you know what? I'm pretty sure that the journey of significance is a lifelong one. There are copious books, films and music written about the pursuit of significance or what so readily is called calling, destiny or purpose (the title of this chapter!). I'm pretty sure people pretend to have it all figured out when in reality they're far from having it sorted.

Freedom from failure

Life is no walk in the park: yup, it's not rocket science either. But it's so easy for us to fall into the trap of thinking the world is against us. The times when these feelings most resonate are when we fail at something (or even feel like we've failed at something when in reality we haven't).

You need to know that failing is totally normal. It doesn't mean you're some insignificant, useless failure at life and everything you touch. It's just part of daily life. We need to change our attitude towards it! I once watched a really inspiring video where a girl in her 20s was talking about growing up in a home where her father encouraged her to share something she failed at each day. Imagine that?! It's funny, isn't it, because we're so used to talking about all the positive things going on in our lives (to seem superior, sorted and successful) that talking about our failures is so out of the ordinary. But I think that's the point! It sounds ludicrous, but it changes our perspective to embrace the normality of failure and seize the chance to learn something from it each time it's experienced. This ultimately turns our failures into something out of the ordinary, extraordinary.

Who you are is not your failures. You are so much more than that.

We're talking about failure, yet I think what makes us feel we have failed is whatever we don't succeed in . . . does that make sense? I mean, 'failure' is an antonym to 'success'. So I want to take us on a journey to what it actually means to succeed . . .

Simplifying success

Why am I bothering to talk about success? Well, it's actually because it's such a focal point in our world. Everyone has slightly different approaches to life, but each approach is a different means to reach success. Our teachers, family, friends, social media world and bosses will all look us in the eye at some point in life and ponder whether or not we are successful (probably). I don't say that to freak you out or send your thoughts into a spiral of despair – I promise!! I'm telling you that because you need to be strong and you need to be firm. You need to know what success is for you personally. You need to know this so that you can be secure with your decisions and behaviour when in communication with other people.

When I looked in the *Oxford English Dictionary*, these were the top two definitions of 'success':

> **The accomplishment of an aim or purpose.**
> **The attainment of fame, wealth, or social status.**

I find it so INTRIGUING that they are two totally different approaches to success! The first one is pretty general and achievable by everyone because it's dependent upon a personal aim or purpose. The second one is pretty self-absorbed and I DON'T like it. You can like it if you want. But I think it's silly. And I think our world is slowly moving away from placing this so highly. People are realizing that fame, wealth and social status don't necessarily bring happiness, contentment or joy. Rather, they just create a continuing desire for more and more . . .

How we define success affects how we wake up in the morning. It influences our approach to life, our behaviour and our decisions. Usually, our definition of success is tightly connected to our values.

Check out these alternative definitions of success:

Never let the fear of

STRIKING OUT

keep you from playing

the game

Babe Ruth

Success is doing your best.
Success is setting goals.
Success believes that you can do it.
Success is balancing work with passion.
Success is overcoming your fears.
Success is following what you believe in.

I wonder what your thoughts are with regard to those ideas! Feel free to scribble them in your journal, doodle round them, choose your favourite and cross out the ones that don't resonate with you. It's pretty important to suss out what is you and what isn't you. Hopefully you will find this a helpful start!

I used to be driven by monetary gain. It was exhausting! And it was because I cared so much about what other people thought about me. It took quite a lot for me to create the shift in my life that was so desperately needed. If I were to define success for me nowadays, it would be the following:

Success is living a passionate and adventurous life.

Passion is a pretty strong emotion. Passion is about doing something wholeheartedly, lovingly and excitedly. I want to be driven. I want to be passionate in my work and home life, in my relationships with family and friends. I want passion to run through the veins of all that I do. This means that I say yes to what makes me passionate and no to what waters down passion. I want to live adventurously. This is because I don't think life is meant to be boring or dull (simple, yes!). My friends all know me for talking about the fact that life is such an adventure! I always say that it's about the journey, not the destination: and I truly do believe that! I don't want to strive for safety; I want to be driven by things that require daring, bold and courageous choices.

Knowing that, for me, success is living a passionate and adventurous life means that I can live confident of what I want to 'achieve' and confident about what doesn't matter to me.

What matters to you?

Often when it comes to our purpose we overcomplicate things. We think that purpose is some 'far-off' idea when, usually, it's a combination of things that matter to us and set our heart aflame with passion.

Relating to resilience

Surprisingly, I look back at my school life and realize that the word 'resilience' was never used to describe me or to refer to me. Yet I think it's one of the most important words in any person's vocabulary.

If you want to imagine a picture or an item that describes the word 'resilience' then think of an elastic band. Resilience puts elasticity back into our everyday lives: elasticity that helps us to spring back into action when something knocks us back or stretches our capacity too far. Resilience helps us to get back up after a failure knocks us down.

Resilience is required by everyday people, but there are also SO many famous people who we all know about who have journeyed through failure and resilience to get to where they are today, to conquer what their life desire was all about. Here are just a few of them:

Albert Einstein He couldn't speak until he was four years old. His teachers and his family thought he was lazy and he was criticized for always asking baffling questions. Yet he proved everyone wrong. He has made groundbreaking progress in science and is now known all over the world for his scientific genius-ness.

Jim Carrey He dropped out of school at the age of 15 to help to support his family. They became homeless for a period of time. It looked as if he could never achieve his dream to be an entertainer. Yet he persevered and is now known as one of the best comedic actors.

Bethany Hamilton She was an incredible surfer when she was attacked by a shark at the age of 13 and lost her arm. A few weeks later she was back on her surfboard and has collected many awards and won many competitions since. A film was even made about her story!

Oprah Winfrey She had an extremely difficult childhood, being abused as a little girl. But in no way was this the end of her story. She was resilient in her education and passion to speak. She is now known as a producer, actress and talk show host.

J. K. Rowling She was rejected by 12 different publishers after writing her first book. She was told she wouldn't be successful as a writer. Yet the Harry Potter series has been a worldwide phenomenon.

> **It is impossible to live without failing at something, unless you live so cautiously that you might as well not have lived at all, in which case you have failed by default.**
>
> (J. K. Rowling)

What a woman. I love what she says. I love how much it ties in with our view of success and, ultimately, our view of life! Our definition of success and our view of life need space for failure and resilience for us to bounce back.

This mindset points to nothing but FREEDOM. When we are free we aren't bound by anything. We aren't bound by failures, mistakes and perfection: that isn't the life we were created to live. We need to accept that and strive for that! We strive for freedom. Freedom so passionately striven for by previous generations of women. And, I hope, passionately striven for by generations yet to come. It starts with you!

Tips and tricks

- ☆ Brainstorm a map of things that matter to you that you're passionate about.
- ☆ Write down a definition of success for you (or even words that relate).

Again, here's my most favourite EVER Bible verse:

> **For you are God's MASTERPIECE, created anew in Christ Jesus to do the good things he planned for you long ago.**
>
> **(Ephesians 2.10)**

So, let's go back over what we've explored in this chapter but this time let's go back over it through the lens of seeing ourselves as a masterpiece.

Am I what has happened to me?

Although our experiences are real, we are more than our experiences. Our experiences are not nearly as powerful as our memories. We are not the sum total of those experiences. The moment we define ourselves by our experiences, we have lost our way. We have to be informed by our experiences but not controlled by them. What has happened to us is not nearly as powerful as our interpretation of them. I'll explain what I mean (or more accurately, writer and pastor Erwin McManus will):

> **Your remembered self is your translation of life. It is the why to all the what. Our interpretation of life determines the material from which we will build the future.**

OK, so that's a little confusing. Basically, the way we explain (and remember) something that has happened to us will

You're braver, bolder and brighter than you think

determine how we feel about it and therefore how we react to it (whether that's positive or negative). But that's exciting, right?! It takes us away from present, temporary events and widens the horizons of our mind to dream, to build, to grow!

The way we interpret what happens in our lives affects the masterpiece that we allow ourselves to become or not become. Our lives are a mosaic of our triumphs and struggles. Do we let our struggles restrain or refocus us? Do we define them or are we defined by them? Do they fill us with dread or hope?

In his book *The Artisan Soul*, Erwin McManus also talks about how our personal happiness is rooted in our remembered self rather than our experienced self: our remembered self (aka our memories) controls how we perceive and experience life. I know that, in troubles, if I don't see myself through a godly lens (the way God sees me) then I feel rubbish, useless and empty. But through a godly lens I can see hope, life and thankfulness despite my experiences.

Romans 5.3–5 expresses how troubles produce perseverance, perseverance develops character and character produces hope: a hope that is firmly rooted in God's promises to never leave us or forsake us. So often when life's challenges come our way we cannot help but be shaken. But when the roots of a tree are deep, there is no reason to fear the wind. So what are our roots sunk deep into? Are they sunk into the promises of God and the truth about who we are?

Am I happy?

Sometimes it's difficult to view ourselves as a masterpiece because of the way things make us feel. But God has given us everything we need to live a godly life in the assurance that we are a masterpiece. What I find helpful when I'm in those moments of doubt, unhappiness, worry, anxiety and fear is knowing what God says about these things. To find this out, we look at the one place that never contradicts the view of God: the Bible.

Happiness

Psalm 16.11 'You will fill me with joy in your presence' – when we spend time with God, he fills us with joy. Joy is more fulfilling than happiness; it doesn't depend on what happens to us.

Worry

Matthew 6.33–34 'But seek first his kingdom and his righteousness, and all these things will be given to you as well. Therefore do not worry about tomorrow, for tomorrow will worry about itself. Each day has enough trouble of its own' – focus on the present day in front of you; God is with you and will guide you.

Anxiety

Philippians 4.6 'Do not be anxious about anything, but in every situation, by prayer and petition, with thanksgiving, present your requests to God' – wake up in the morning and offer your day to God; he cares about your anxieties.

Fear

Isaiah 41.10 'So do not fear, for I am with you; do not be dismayed, for I am your God. I will strengthen you and help you . . .' – even when it doesn't feel like it, God is with you and he is working through you.

Am I significant?

Our lives will be a tapestry of failures and success. Resilience is the key to 'keeping calm and carrying on'.

The strength, perseverance and courage we embed into our lives will determine the craftsmanship of the lives we create. Building our lives as masterpieces demands the journey of a lifetime: a journey of both failure and success. We know that God has instilled purpose and passion in our hearts, but as self-help author Steve Pavlina wrote, 'When you live for a strong purpose, then hard work isn't an option, it's a necessity.' We have to persevere in running the marathon we have been called to run (despite our circumstances) for such a time as this.

You are a masterpiece: the most beautifully crafted artwork.

I know I'm guilty of wanting to be the most beautifully created artwork instantaneously and immediately. This is perhaps a danger brought about by social media: it's all about present, consumeristic, instant access. It prides itself on immediate creativity, beauty, inspiration and imagination illustrated by a masterpiece. Yet the creation of a masterpiece also demands words like 'resilience', 'tenacity', 'discipline' and 'perseverance'.

Each of us is unique in our passions and purpose and has been gifted with the unique materials with which to pursue craftsmanship in our lives: only requiring strength and courage from the depths of our heart to choose who we become.

The gold at the end of the rainbow

I think we spend so much time longing for the pot of gold at the end of the rainbow that we forget that golden moments aren't about a destination, but that every moment (even bad ones) has golden opportunities. Kintsukuroi is the Japanese art of repairing cracked pottery with gold or silver with the understanding that it is more beautiful for having been broken. I love the imagery of pouring gold into every moment and situation and I like to think that's God's role in our lives. What a beautiful perspective to have!

You may be feeling like you're cracked pottery. You may feel like you've messed up. You may feel empty or shameful. You may feel desperate for God to turn your brokenness into gold.

My advice to you would be to try to work through what is making you feel broken. Often when we acknowledge things for what they are, they start to lose their power over us. It's a work in progress but it leads to freedom.

I find journalling a really helpful method for putting my thoughts, experiences, confusions, worries and hurts all down on paper. I would then encourage praying through it with God because he is our ultimate helper (and with someone else whom you trust, if you're able). He is the one who holds the ultimate truth about us and our circumstances. If you feel like you're broken, read his truth in Psalm 34.18, Isaiah 43.2 and Psalm 46.1. He is the one who already sees all the gold in us, and longs to communicate what that is to us. He longs to turn our broken struggle into our hope-filled story. It may take time. It may take handing it over to him multiple times. But he is with you through it all.

Girls, whatever happens to you, know that God is a God who is pouring gold into your situation. He is a God that turns things for good (Romans 8.28). He is turning your brokenness into beauty.

Here's a prayer for you to pray when you feel in need:

> God, I feel broken. I cannot do this without you. You are my creator. Please take my brokenness and gift me with your help, love, truth, strength and joy. Stay close to me and hold me in your arms. Show yourself to me and restore the life you created for me. Amen.

She has *fire* in her soul and

grace in her heart

READY. SET. GO!

You've made it to the final pages of the book! Congrats. Well, that's assuming you've made it . . .

We have journeyed through Value, Beauty and Purpose, yet only just scratched the surface of all there is to know about them. You will walk through moments of your life when your Value, Beauty and Purpose is pretty sussed, and at other times you may freak out and face setbacks on the way. Ultimately, we're all walking our own paths. And my hope and prayer is that this book has encouraged you on yours.

One thing that keeps me on my path is music. Music has the power to take us to a totally new place in our minds; it inspires and draws us into a new reality.

My sister and I absolutely loved Philippa Hanna when we were growing up. She's an inspirational Christian songwriter and every year we used to watch her play at a conference and invited her to our church to run an evening of music! One of her songs really hit home for me, and the video for it is just as powerful.

Let me encourage you to read the lyrics slowly. Read them as total truth about who you are:

> I don't wanna waste anymore time in the mirror
> Watching my face never change
> I don't feel beautiful today
> I don't waste anymore hard earned cash on these 'miracles'
> That never change the way I feel, don't make me beautiful today
> How long can I hide-away beneath this disguise?
> And what drastic measure do I have to take to realise . . .
> That I am amazing, in spite of what I can see,
> When I look at myself wishing I could be anyone other than me
> Cos I was created
> With everything I could ever need
> So I'm not gonna change
> I'm gonna stay just the way God made me.

I think that when God created you to be you, he wished and hoped that you would live knowing how loved, unique, beautiful and treasured you are as his masterpiece.

I also believe that my very few and inexhaustive wishes and hopes for girls (you included!) are a reflection of his heart:

1 that girls can walk down the street without fear of being cat-called;

2. that girls aren't treated differently from boys;
3. that girls aren't restricted by gender stereotypes;
4. that girls aren't judged on their appearance;
5. that girls have a fair, diverse and positive representation in the media;
6. that girls feel empowered in their contexts;
7. that girls move away from competing;
8. that girls don't feel they have to display their body to gain their worth;
9. that girls feel free to be their true selves;
10. that society would support and champion girls across the nation.

Let that list be the driving force of you embracing who you really are and who you are yet to become.

And let this letter that I blogged to my younger self be an encouragement to you:

> *Dear my younger self,*
>
> *Well done. You're navigating life pretty well, believe it or not. You may feel lost, inadequate and confused but that's OK because a lot of other people actually feel that way too. You aren't alone with your feelings and you're not an insignificant life.*
>
> *It's true that 14, 15, 16, etc., are difficult ages. But also super exciting. Try not to get bogged down with grades, boys, popularity and image – you'll soon learn that life is*

so much more than that. It sounds simple but it's one of the most profound mindsets that you can adopt.

Remember that some friends will let you down; people aren't perfect. You may also let them down too. Remember that everyone is just trying their best.

You'll soon think that the perfect image in reality and on social media will give you the ultimate happiness, but I'm sorry to say that it most definitely won't – the validation of others will never prove your worthiness, and perfection itself is an illusion: no one gets there, no one achieves it and no one is sustained by it.

Don't worry – this isn't a dead end. You know that Jesus guy that you've learned so much about but never known personally? Well, you're gonna choose him and he's gonna change everything. He is a constant. He is perfection. He holds the true truth about who you are, not the false truth that the world presents. He is the centre of everything and you're privileged to have a part to play in his master-story because he calls you his masterpiece. What he says counts.

So stand firm and stick in there and seek him first. Soon your struggle will become your story and your passion will be made known to you.

And to top it all off, you'll meet friends who will stick by your side for life. You'll build real friendships that will support you in struggle and you'll celebrate one another's stories. Because every story is an original.

One of the most life-changing things you'll learn is that the world will be so focused on the outward appearance but that won't sustain you. You are so much more than your appearance. Don't strive to be pretty. Strive to be pretty compassionate, pretty humble, pretty patient, pretty passionate and pretty loving. Assess the condition of your heart, not your face or body.

You are enough.

Over time the bruises will begin to heal. And as you get to know God more personally, you'll grow in the assurance that what he says counts. You'll soar. You'll dream. You'll be OK. You'll be more than OK. You'll be doing life with the Creator of life itself. And it has been, is and will continue to be the greatest adventure of all.

Love from your slightly older self.

X

You play a key part in creating the society that we live in today as well as in the future.

Imagine what kind of world we would create if we all stepped up and passionately and courageously sought after value, beauty and purpose for every girl, from every neighbourhood, in every nation and beyond.

The NEXT CHAPTER is

yours to write . . .

This book is only really the beginning, and girl, you write the rest! So, with your pen in your hand . . .

Ready. Set. Go!

YOUR LIFE-KIT

I've just told you 'Ready. Set. Go!' haven't I?! There's one more catch . . .

Along the way, you'll need support. You'll need people and places you can go to for encouragement and a little boost. Think of them like energy tablets; they'll give you what you need to take the next step.

One valid question you are likely to still be asking is 'BUT WHO AM I?' It's a question we ask ourselves almost every day of our existence on Earth, manifesting itself in different ways. There are a few tools I have found unbelievably helpful. These tools look at the character we have been born with and have cultivated over the years. These tools look at how we interact with people and the world around us. These tools opened my eyes to the strength (and weakness!) of who I am, ready to pursue all that God has for me in the world.

StrengthsFinder This tool discovers what you naturally do best, indicating how to develop your greatest talents and live your best life. It will massively improve your self-awareness and it massively increased my confidence to be who I am.

Go to <www.gallupstrengthscenter.com>.

Myers-Briggs This tool is a self-report questionnaire that indicates our different psychological preferences about how we perceive and experience the world and therefore make decisions (i.e. our natural tendency towards introversion or extraversion). The personality profile that it gives you is eye-opening and strengthening.

Go to <www.mbtionline.com>.

Enneagram This tool consists of nine different personality types, used to determine which type is dominant for you. It's another helpful method for self-understanding and self-development, pointing out our unconscious, natural orientations towards life.

Go to <www.electicenergies.com>.

I also wanted to give you some more tools for life, so here are some of the things that I've found helpful at different points in life, all categorized neatly for you:

Websites

Mind: the mental health charity: <www.mind.org.uk>

Think Twice: mental illness awareness: <www.thinktwiceinfo.org>

Youthscape: innovative youth work: <www.youthscape.co.uk>

More Precious: equipping girls' relationship with God: <www.morepecious.co.uk>

Blogs

Girl Got Faith: faith, beauty and lifestyle: <www.girlgotfaith.com>

It's Milk and Honey: lifestyle hub: <www.itsmilkandhoney.com>

Magazines

Magnify: faith, feminism and fashion: <www.hellomagnify.com>

YouTube

Koko: spoken words and videos relating to what young people are facing: <kokostories>

Dove: beauty confidence videos and resources: <DoveUS>

Music

Philippa Hanna

Rend Collective

United Pursuit

Hillsong

Lauren Daigle

Apps

The Bible: choose a plan to work through.

Books

Tim Chester, *Will You Be My Facebook Friend?*, Leyland, Lancs: 10Publishing, 2012.

Robin Ham, *Filtered Grace*, ebook available to download from <https://books.noisetrade.com/robinham/filtered-grace-reflections-on>.

Jenna and Max Lucado, *Redefining Beautiful*, Nashville, TN: Thomas Nelson, 2010.

Max Lucado, *You Are Special*, Oxford: Candle Books, 2004.

Cathy Madavan, *Digging for Diamonds*, Milton Keynes: Authentic Media, 2015.

Carolyn Mahaney and Nicole Whitacre, *True Beauty*, Wheaton, IL: Crossway Books, 2014.

Chine Mbubaegbu, *Am I Beautiful?*, Milton Keynes: Authentic Media, 2013.

Joyce Meyer, *The Confident Woman*, Nashville, TN: Faithwords, 2010.

John Ortberg, *The Me I Want To Be*, Grand Rapids, MI: Zondervan, 2014.

Arianna Walker, *Mirror Image*, Oxenhope, Yorks: Presence Books, 2011.

NOTES

1 See <http://helpmeinvestigate.com/education/2013/04/mapped-how-many-hours-do-children-spend-at-school-around-the-world/>.

2 You have to read it! It's called 'In the spirit of intl women's day' and comes from her collection of poems, *Milk and Honey*. The poem is widely available on the internet.

3 See <https://www.instagram.com/about/us/>

4 It's well worth checking out! See <https://40acts.org.uk/>.

5 See <http://metro.co.uk/2017/04/14/a-quarter-of-young-women-in-the-uk-are-suffering-from-anxiety-and-depression-6574411/>.

6 See <https://www.nspcc.org.uk/what-we-do/news-opinion/anxiety-rising-concern-young-people-contacting-childline/>.

7 See <https://www.psychologytoday.com/blog/the-power-rest/201705/rest-success>.